Untuk Nini
di Kanada

desserts

Dari : Uli, Githa, Tiblo ♥

Nanti sepulang dari Kanada,
kamu sudah harus bisa
masakin desserts² buku ini ya!

desserts

MURDOCH BOOKS

contents

sweet surrender

One of the very best things about being an adult is there's no one to insist that you can't have your pudding if you don't eat all your greens. Who wants to fill up on peas, spinach or cabbage if there's something sweet waiting to be devoured next?

Another fabulous aspect of adulthood is that you can conjure the desserts of your very dreams, any time (and as frequently) as you wish. The possibilities are deliciously endless. Is it something simple, seasonal and fruity you fancy? Then peaches with panettone or pineapple with brown sugar and toasted coconut might just fit the bill. Or does the occasion, and the climate, call for something decidedly chilled-out? Ice cream and sorbet taste infinitely better when they're home-made as do granita, mousse and trifle. As if that's not confusing choice enough, there are all those comforting, baked goodies to consider. These are desserts which never go out of date, style or favour; in this happy group belong the likes of bread and butter pudding, plum cobbler, apple crumble and pies in all their crusty, tender glory.

Arguably the ultimate category of dessert though is the rich type. These sweets involve unapologetic quantities of cream, chocolate, eggs, butter, mascarpone cheese and the like. Many have alluringly foreign names like zabaglione, panna cotta, tiramisu and crème brûlée and they're all completely irresistible. The Brussels sprouts really don't stand a chance.

fruity

Lemon grass and ginger infused fruit salad

60 g (2¼ oz/¼ cup) caster (superfine) sugar
2 cm x 2 cm (¾ inch x ¾ inch) piece fresh ginger, thinly sliced
1 lemon grass stem, bruised and halved
1 large passionfruit
1 red pawpaw
½ honeydew melon
1 large mango
1 small pineapple
12 fresh lychees
5 g (⅛ oz) mint leaves, shredded

Put the sugar, ginger and lemon grass in a small saucepan, add 125 ml (4 fl oz/
½ cup) of water and stir over low heat to dissolve the sugar. Boil for 5 minutes,
or until reduced to about 4 tablespoons. Allow to cool. Strain the syrup and add
the passionfruit pulp.

Peel and seed the pawpaw and melon. Cut into 4 cm (1½ inch) cubes. Peel the
mango and cut the flesh into cubes, discarding the stone. Peel, halve and core the
pineapple and cut into cubes. Peel the lychees, then make a slit in the flesh and
remove the seed.

Place all the fruit in a large serving bowl. Pour the syrup over and garnish with the
shredded mint.

SERVES 4

Poached pears in
saffron citrus syrup

1 vanilla bean
½ teaspoon saffron threads
185 g (6½ oz/¾ cup) caster (superfine) sugar
2 teaspoons grated lemon zest
4 pears, peeled, stalks intact
whipped cream, to serve (optional)
biscotti, to serve (optional)

Put the vanilla bean, saffron threads, caster sugar and lemon zest in a saucepan with 1 litre (35 fl oz/4 cups) of water and mix well. Stir over low heat until the sugar dissolves. Bring to the boil, then reduce the heat and simmer for 10 12 minutes, or until slightly reduced and syrupy.

Add the pears and cook, covered, for 12–15 minutes, or until tender when tested with a metal skewer. Turn the pears over with a slotted spoon halfway through cooking. Once cooked, remove from the syrup.

Bring the syrup to the boil, and cook for 10 minutes, or until the syrup has reduced by half and thickened slightly. Remove the vanilla bean and drizzle the syrup over the pears. Serve with whipped cream and biscotti, if desired.

SERVES 4

Red fruit salad
with berries

Syrup
60 g (2¼ oz/¼ cup) caster (superfine) sugar
125 ml (4 fl oz/½ cup) dry red wine
1 star anise
1 teaspoon finely chopped lemon zest

250 g (9 oz/1⅔ cups) strawberries, hulled and halved
150 g (5½ oz/1 cup) blueberries
150 g (5½ oz/1¼ cups) raspberries, mulberries or other red berries
250 g (9 oz) cherries
5 small red plums (about 250 g/9 oz), stones removed and quartered
plain yoghurt, to serve

To make the syrup, place the sugar, wine, star anise, lemon zest and 125 ml (4 fl oz/ ½ cup) of water in a small saucepan. Bring to the boil over medium heat, stirring to dissolve the sugar. Boil the syrup for 3 minutes, then set aside to cool for 30 minutes. When cool, strain the syrup.

Mix the fruit together in a large bowl and pour on the red wine syrup. Mix well to coat the fruit in the syrup and refrigerate for 1 hour 30 minutes. Serve the fruit with some syrup and the yoghurt.

SERVES 6

Peaches cardinal

4 large ripe peaches
300 g (10½ oz/2½ cups) raspberries
2 teaspoons icing (confectioners') sugar, plus extra, to dust

If the peaches are very ripe, put them in a bowl and pour boiling water over them. Leave for 1 minute, then drain and carefully peel away the skin. If the fruit you have is not so ripe, dissolve 2 tablespoons of sugar in a saucepan of water, add the peaches and cover the pan. Gently poach the peaches for 5–10 minutes, or until tender. Drain and peel.

Allow the peaches cool, then halve each one and remove the stone. Put two halves in each serving glass. Put the raspberries in a food processor or blender and mix until puréed. Pass through a fine nylon sieve to get rid of the seeds.

Sift the icing sugar over the raspberry purée and stir in. Drizzle the purée over the peaches, cover and chill thoroughly. Dust a little icing sugar over the top to serve.

SERVES 4

Strawberries with balsamic vinegar

750 g (1 lb 10 oz) ripe small strawberries
60 g (2¼ oz/¼ cup) caster (superfine) sugar
2 tablespoons balsamic vinegar
125 g (4 fl oz/½ cup) mascarpone

Wipe the strawberries with a clean damp cloth and carefully remove the green stalks. If the strawberries are large, cut each one in half.

Place all the strawberries in a large glass bowl, sprinkle the caster sugar evenly over the top and toss gently to coat. Set aside for 2 hours to macerate, then sprinkle the balsamic vinegar over the strawberries. Toss again, then refrigerate for 30 minutes.

Spoon the strawberries into four glasses, drizzle with the syrup and top with a dollop of mascarpone.

SERVES 4

NOTE: If you leave the strawberries to macerate for more than 2 hours, it is best to refrigerate them.

Apricots in cardamom syrup

300 g (10½ oz/1⅔ cups) dried apricots
3 tablespoons caster (superfine) sugar
3 tablespoons slivered, blanched almonds
1 cm (½ inch) piece of ginger, sliced
4 cardamom pods
1 cinnamon stick
4 pieces edible silver leaf (varak), optional

Soak the apricots in 750 ml (26 fl oz/3 cups) of water in a large saucepan for 4 hours, or until plumped up.

Add the caster sugar, almonds, ginger, cardamom and cinnamon to the apricots and bring slowly to the boil, stirring until the sugar has dissolved. Reduce the heat to a simmer and cook until the liquid has reduced by half and formed a thick syrup. Pour into a bowl, then refrigerate.

Serve in small bowls with a piece of silver leaf for decoration, if desired. To do this, invert the piece of backing paper over each bowl. As soon as the silver leaf touches the apricots it will come away from the backing and stick to them.

SERVES 4

Fruit skewers with rum butter

1 peach, peeled, stoned and cut into 8 pieces
1 mango, peeled, stoned and cut into 8 pieces
8 strawberries, hulled and halved
160 g (5½ oz) papaya, cut into 8 pieces
160 g (5½ oz) pineapple, cut into 8 pieces
2 bananas, cut into 2 cm (¾ inch) pieces
185 ml (6 fl oz/¾ cup) dark rum
60 g (2¼ oz/⅓ cup) dark brown sugar
20 g (¾ oz) butter
ice cream, to serve

Put the peach, mango, strawberries, papaya, pineapple and banana in a bowl with the rum and sugar. Gently mix to combine until all of the fruit is coated in the marinade. Cover and refrigerate for 1 hour.

Meanwhile, soak eight wooden skewers in cold water for 1 hour.

Drain the marinade into a heavy-based saucepan and thread the fruit onto the skewers.

Bring the marinade to the boil over medium heat, then reduce the heat and simmer for 5 minutes, or until it is reduced and syrupy. Remove from the heat and whisk in the butter until smooth and glossy.

Preheat a flat barbecue grill plate to medium direct heat. Cook the skewers for 5–8 minutes on each side, or until they are golden, basting all over with the rum glaze during the last minute of cooking. Drizzle the skewers with the rum glaze and serve warm with ice cream.

SERVES 4

Spiced poached pears

6 beurre bosc pears, peeled, halved and cored
300 ml (10½ fl oz) rosé wine
150 ml (5 fl oz) apple or pear juice
4 cloves
1 vanilla bean, halved
1 cinnamon stick
1 tablespoon maple syrup
200 g (7 oz) low-fat vanilla yoghurt

Put the pears in a deep frying pan with a lid, over medium heat, and add the wine, fruit juice and cloves. Scrape the seeds out of the vanilla bean and add both the seeds and pod to the pan. Stir in the cinnamon stick and maple syrup. Bring to the boil, then reduce the heat and simmer for 5–7 minutes, or until the pears are tender. Remove from the heat and cover with the lid.

Leave for 30 minutes to allow the flavours to infuse, then remove the pears with a slotted spoon and set aside. Return the syrup to the heat and boil for 6–8 minutes, or until reduced by half. Strain the syrup over the pears and serve warm or chilled with the yoghurt.

SERVES 6

Spiced fruit salad

110 g (3¾ oz/½ cup) caster (superfine) sugar
4 slices ginger
1 bird's eye chilli, cut in half
juice and zest of 2 limes
fruit, such as a mixture of watermelon, melon,
    mango, banana, cherries, lychees, kiwi fruit
    (enough for 4 portions)

Put the sugar in a saucepan over medium heat and add 125 ml (4 fl oz/½ cup) of water and the ginger and chilli. Heat until the sugar melts, then leave to cool. Add the lime juice and zest. Remove the ginger and chilli.

Put the fruit into a bowl and pour the syrup over. Leave to marinate in the fridge for 30 minutes. Serve with ice cream or sorbet, if desired.

SERVES 4

Orchard fruit compote

90 g (3¼ oz/¼ cup) honey
½ teaspoon ground ginger
1 cinnamon stick
3 whole cloves
pinch ground nutmeg
750 ml (26 fl oz/3 cups) dessert
     wine, such as Sauternes
1 lemon

6 pitted prunes
3 dried peaches, halved
5 dates, seeded and halved
10 dried apricots
1 lapsang souchong tea bag
2 golden delicious apples
2 beurre bosc pears
400 g (14 oz) plain yoghurt

Put the honey, ginger, cinnamon stick, cloves, nutmeg and wine in a saucepan. Peel a large piece of zest from the lemon and place in the pan. Squeeze the juice from the lemon to give 3 tablespoons of juice and add to the pan. Bring to the boil, stirring, then simmer for 20 minutes.

Meanwhile, put the prunes, peaches, dates and apricots in a large heatproof bowl. Cover with boiling water, add the tea bag and leave to soak.

Peel and core the apples and pears, and cut into pieces about the same size as the dried fruits. Add to the syrup and simmer for 8–10 minutes, or until tender. Drain the dried fruit and remove the tea bag. Add the fruit to the pan and cook for a further 5 minutes.

Remove all the fruit from the pan with a slotted spoon and set aside. Return the pan to the heat, bring to the boil, then reduce the heat and simmer for 6 minutes, or until the syrup has reduced by half. Pour over the fruit compote and chill for 30 minutes. Serve with the yoghurt.

SERVES 4

Fruit poached in red wine

3 pears, peeled, quartered and cored
3 apples, peeled, quartered and cored
50 g (1¾ oz) sugar
1 vanilla pod, cut in half lengthways
2 small cinnamon sticks
400 ml (14 fl oz) red wine
200 ml (7 fl oz) dessert wine or port
700 g (1 lb 9 oz) red-skinned plums, halved

Put the pears and apples in a large saucepan. Add the sugar, vanilla pod, cinnamon sticks, red wine and dessert wine and bring to the boil. Reduce the heat and gently simmer for about 5–10 minutes, or until just soft.

Add the plums, stirring them through the pears and apples, and bring the liquid back to a simmer. Cook for a further 5 minutes, or until the plums are soft.

Remove the saucepan from the heat, cover with a lid and leave the fruit to marinate in the syrup for at least 6 hours. Reheat gently to serve warm or serve at room temperature with cream or ice cream and a biscuit (cookie).

SERVES 6

Summer fruit compote

500 g (1 lb 2 oz/2 cups) caster (superfine) sugar
750 ml (26 fl oz/3 cups) white wine, such as Chardonnay
2 teaspoons finely grated lime zest
3 tablespoons lime juice
2 mangoes
3 freestone peaches
3 nectarines
vanilla ice cream, to serve

Put the sugar, white wine, lime zest and juice in a large saucepan over low heat. Stir for 3 minutes, or until the sugar has dissolved. Bring to the boil, then reduce the heat and simmer for 2 minutes. Keep warm.

Cut the cheeks from the mangoes, then remove the skin. Cut each mango cheek into 6 thick wedges. Place the mango in a large bowl.

Cut a cross in one end of the peaches and nectarines, and plunge into a bowl of boiling water, and then into cold water. Peel and cut into 4 wedges each, discarding the stones. Add to the mango.

Pour the warm syrup over the fruit, and refrigerate, covered, for 2–3 hours. To serve, return to room temperature and serve with ice cream.

SERVES 6

NOTE: You can leave the peaches and nectarines unpeeled, if preferred.

Peaches poached in wine

4 just-ripe yellow-fleshed freestone peaches
500 ml (17 fl oz/2 cups) sweet white wine,
    such as Sauternes
3 tablespoons orange liqueur
1 cinnamon stick
250 g (9 oz) sugar
1 vanilla bean, split
8 mint leaves
mascarpone or crème fraîche, to serve

Cut a small cross in the base of each peach. Immerse the peaches in boiling water for 30 seconds, then drain and cool slightly. Peel off the skin, cut in half and carefully remove the stones.

Put the wine, liqueur, cinnamon stick, sugar and vanilla bean in a deep frying pan large enough to hold the peach haves in a single layer. Heat, stirring, until the sugar dissolves. Bring to the boil, then reduce the heat and simmer for 5 minutes. Add the peaches and simmer for 4 minutes, turning them halfway. Remove with a slotted spoon. Simmer the syrup for 6–8 minutes, or until thick. Strain.

Arrange the peaches on a platter, cut side up. Spoon the syrup over the top and garnish each half with a mint leaf. Serve the peaches warm or chilled with a dollop of mascarpone or crème fraîche.

SERVES 4

Pineapple with sugar glaze and toasted coconut

1 pineapple
95 g (3¼ oz/½ cup) dark brown sugar
½ teaspoon natural vanilla extract
1 tablespoon Galliano
60 g (2¼ oz) butter
2 tablespoons coconut flakes, toasted
vanilla ice cream, to serve

Peel the pineapple and remove all the eyes, then slice it lengthways into quarters and remove the core. Cut into long 1 cm (½ inch) wide wedges.

Put the brown sugar, vanilla extract and 2 teaspoons of water in a small saucepan over medium heat. Cook for 5 minutes, or until the sugar has dissolved. Remove from the heat and add the Galliano. Return the pan to the heat and simmer for 3 minutes. Whisk in the butter and continue to simmer over low heat for 15 minutes, or until smooth and thick.

Preheat a barbecue chargrill plate to medium direct heat. Brush the pineapple with the brown sugar glaze and grill for 2–3 minutes, or until grill marks appear. Arrange the pineapple pieces in a large bowl, top with the glaze and the toasted coconut and serve with vanilla ice cream.

SERVES 6

Grilled figs with ricotta

2 tablespoons honey
1 cinnamon stick
3 tablespoons flaked almonds
4 large (or 8 small) fresh figs
125 g (4½ oz/½ cup) ricotta cheese
½ teaspoon natural vanilla extract
2 tablespoons icing (confectioners') sugar, sifted
pinch ground cinnamon
½ teaspoon finely grated orange zest

Put the honey and cinnamon stick in a saucepan with 4 tablespoons of water. Bring to the boil, then reduce the heat and simmer gently for 6 minutes, or until thickened and reduced by half. Discard the cinnamon stick and stir in the almonds.

Preheat the grill (broiler) to hot and grease a shallow ovenproof dish large enough to fit all the figs side by side. Slice the figs into quarters from the top to within 1 cm (½ inch) of the bottom, keeping them attached at the base. Arrange in the prepared dish.

Combine the ricotta, vanilla, icing sugar, ground cinnamon and orange zest in a small bowl. Divide the filling among the figs, spooning it into their cavities. Spoon the syrup over the top. Put under the grill and cook until the juices start to come out from the figs and the almonds are lightly toasted. Cool for 2–3 minutes. Spoon the juices and any fallen almonds from the bottom of the dish over the figs and serve immediately.

SERVES 4

Winter fruit in orange ginger syrup

60 g (2¼ oz/¼ cup) caster (superfine) sugar
3 tablespoons orange juice
2 strips orange zest
1 cinnamon stick
250 g (9 oz) dried fruit salad, large pieces cut in half
100 g (3½ oz) pitted dried dates
1 teaspoon grated fresh ginger
200 g (7 oz) low-fat plain yoghurt

Put the caster sugar, orange juice, orange zest, cinnamon stick and 375 ml (13 fl oz/ 1½ cups) of water in a large saucepan over low heat. Stir until the caster sugar dissolves, then increase the heat and simmer, without stirring, for 5 minutes, or until the syrup mixture has thickened slightly.

Add the dried fruit salad, dates and ginger, and mix well. Cover and simmer over low heat for 5 minutes, or until the fruit has softened. Remove from the heat and set aside, covered, for 5 minutes. Discard the orange zest and cinnamon stick. If serving cold, remove from the saucepan and allow to cool.

Put the fruits in a bowl and drizzle a little of the syrup over the top. Serve with the yoghurt.

SERVES 4

Summer pudding

150 g (5½ oz) blackcurrants
150 g (5½ oz) redcurrants
150 g (5½ oz) raspberries
150 g (5½ oz) blackberries
200 g (7 oz) strawberries, hulled and quartered or halved
125 g (4½ oz/½ cup) caster (superfine) sugar, or to taste
6–8 slices sliced white bread, crusts removed
thick (double/heavy) cream, to serve (optional)

Put all the berries except the strawberries in a saucepan with 125 ml (4 fl oz/ ½ cup) of water and heat for 5 minutes, or until the berries begin to soften. Add the strawberries and remove from the heat. Add sugar, to taste. Allow to cool.

Line six 170 ml (5½ fl oz/⅔ cup) moulds or a 1 litre (35 fl oz/4 cup) pudding basin with the bread. For the small moulds cut a circle to fit the bottom and strips to fit around the sides. For the basin, cut a large circle out of one slice for the bottom and cut the rest of the bread into strips to fit the side. Drain a little of the juice off the fruit. Dip one side of each piece of bread in the juice before fitting it, juice side down, into the basin, leaving no gaps. Do not squeeze the bread or it will not absorb the juice.

Fill each mould with fruit and add some juice. Cover the top with the remaining dipped bread, juice-side up. Cover with plastic wrap. For the small moulds, sit a small tin on top of each. For the basin, sit a small plate onto the plastic wrap, then weigh it down with a large tin. Place on a tray to catch any juice which may overflow, and chill overnight. Carefully turn out the pudding and serve with leftover fruit mixture and cream, if desired.

SERVES 6

Grilled peaches
with panettone

125 g (4½ oz/½ cup) caster (superfine) sugar
½ vanilla bean, halved and scraped
1 tablespoon Grand Marnier
4 ripe peaches
oil, for brushing
4 large slices panettone
80 g (2¾ oz/⅓ cup) crème fraîche

Put the sugar, vanilla bean and 3 tablespoons of water in a saucepan and stir over low heat until the sugar has dissolved. Simmer the mixture, without stirring, for 10 minutes, then remove from the heat. Stir in the Grand Marnier and keep warm.

Dip the peaches into a saucepan of boiling water for 5 seconds, then refresh them under cold water and remove the skins, which should slip off easily. Cut the peaches in half, remove the stone and lightly brush the cut side with oil.

Preheat a barbecue chargrill plate to medium direct heat and grill the peaches, cut side down, for 5 minutes, or until golden and warmed through. Grill the panettone for 1 minute on each side, or until it is marked and lightly toasted. The panettone will brown very quickly, so be careful to not burn it.

Arrange the grilled peaches over the panettone, drizzle with the vanilla syrup and serve with a scoop of crème fraîche.

SERVES 4

chilled

Apple and pear sorbet

4 large green apples, peeled, cored and chopped
4 pears, peeled, cored and chopped
1 piece of lemon zest (1.5 cm x 4 cm/⅝ inch x 1½ inch)
1 cinnamon stick
3 tablespoons lemon juice
4 tablespoons caster (superfine) sugar
2 tablespoons Calvados or poire William liqueur, optional

Place the apple and pear in a large deep saucepan with the lemon zest, cinnamon stick and enough water to just cover the fruit. Cover and poach the fruit gently over medium heat for 6–8 minutes, or until tender. Remove the lemon zest and cinnamon stick. Place the fruit in a food processor and blend with the lemon juice until smooth.

Place the sugar in a saucepan with 4 tablespoons water, bring to the boil and simmer for 1 minute. Add the fruit purée and the liqueur and combine.

Pour into a shallow metal tray and freeze for 2 hours, or until the mixture is frozen around the edges. Transfer to a food processor or bowl and blend or beat until just smooth. Pour back into the tray and return to the freezer. Repeat this process three times. For the final freezing, place in an airtight container, cover the surface with a piece of greaseproof paper and cover with a lid. Serve in small glasses or bowls.

SERVES 4–6

NOTE: Pour an extra nip of Calvados over the sorbet to serve, if desired.

Cassata

30 g (1 oz) crystallised ginger, finely chopped
50 g (¼ oz) red glacé cherries, roughly chopped or sliced
300 g (10½ oz) low-fat vanilla ice cream, softened
250 g (9 oz) frozen strawberry fruit dessert, softened
300 g (10½ oz) low-fat chocolate ice cream, softened

Line a 1.25 litre (44 fl oz/5 cup) rectangular tin with plastic wrap, leaving an overhang on the sides.

Stir the ginger and glacé cherries into the vanilla ice cream until well combined. Spoon into the prepared tin and smooth down. Freeze for 1 hour, or until firm.

Spoon the strawberry fruit dessert over the ice cream mixture, smooth the surface and return to the freezer for another hour.

Spoon the chocolate ice cream over the strawberry, smoothing the surface. Cover with plastic wrap, and freeze for at least 3 hours or overnight. To serve, plunge the bottom of the tin into warm water for 10 seconds to loosen and lift out using the plastic wrap. Cut into slices and serve.

SERVES 10–12

Coffee granita

200 g (9 oz/1 cup) caster (superfine) sugar
1.25 litres (44 fl oz/5 cups) very strong espresso coffee

Heat the caster sugar with 25 ml (1 fl oz) of hot water in a saucepan until the sugar dissolves. Simmer for 3 minutes to make a sugar syrup. Add the coffee and stir well.

Pour the mixture into a plastic or metal freezer box. The mixture should be no deeper than 3 cm (1¼ inch) so that the granita freezes quickly and breaks up easily. Stir every 2 hours with a fork to break up the ice crystals as they form repeat this two or three times. The granita is ready when almost set but still grainy. Stir a fork through it just before serving.

SERVES 6

White chocolate mousse

100 g (3½ oz) white chocolate melts (buttons)
125 ml (4 fl oz/½ cup) skim milk
2 teaspoons gelatine
400 g (14 oz) low-fat French vanilla fromage frais or
   whipped yoghurt
3 egg whites
3 tablespoons passionfruit pulp
icing (confectioners') sugar, to dust

Put the chocolate and milk in a small saucepan and stir over low heat until the chocolate has melted. Allow to cool. Place 3 tablespoons of boiling water in a heatproof bowl, sprinkle evenly with the gelatine, and stir until dissolved. Using a wooden spoon, stir the gelatine into the chocolate mixture.

Put the fromage frais in a large bowl and gradually stir in the chocolate mixture, a little at a time, stirring until smooth.

Beat the egg whites in a dry bowl using electric beaters until soft peaks form. Gently fold the egg whites and the passionfruit pulp into the chocolate mixture. Divide the mixture equally among eight 125 ml (4 fl oz/½ cup) serving dishes or a 1 litre (35 fl oz/4 cup) glass bowl. Refrigerate for 3 hours, or until set. Serve with a light dusting of icing sugar.

SERVES 8

NOTE: It is important to have the ingredients at room temperature to ensure the texture is smooth.

Mango sorbet

375 g (13 oz/1½ cups) caster (superfine) sugar
125 ml (4 fl oz/½ cup) lime juice
5 fresh mangoes

Put the sugar in a saucepan with 625 ml (21½ fl oz/2½ cups) of water. Stir over low heat until the sugar dissolves, then bring to the boil. Reduce to a simmer for 15 minutes, then stir in the juice.

Peel the mangoes and remove the flesh from the stone. Chop and put in a heatproof bowl. Add the syrup and leave to cool.

Put the mango mixture in a blender and blend until smooth. Pour into a shallow metal dish and freeze for 1 hour, or until it starts to freeze around the edges. Return to the blender and blend until smooth. Pour back into the tray and return to the freezer. Repeat three times. For the final freezing, place in an airtight container and cover the sorbet with a piece of greaseproof paper and lid. Allow the sorbet to soften slightly before serving with tropical fruit.

SERVES 4

NOTE: You can use frozen mango if fresh is unavailable. Use 1 kg (2 lb 4 oz) frozen mango cheeks, softened, 185 g (6½ oz/¾ cup) caster (superfine) sugar and 3 tablespoons of lime juice, and follow the method as above.

Passionfruit mousse

5–6 passionfruit
6 eggs, separated
185 g (6½ oz/¾ cup) caster (superfine) sugar
½ teaspoon finely grated lemon zest
3 tablespoons lemon juice
1 tablespoon gelatine
315 ml (10¾ fl oz/1¼ cups) pouring (whipping) cream,
    lightly whipped
40 g (1½ oz/¾ cup) flaked coconut, toasted

Cut the passionfruit in half and scoop out the pulp. Strain, then measure out
3 tablespoons of juice and set aside. Add the seeds and pulp to the remaining juice
and set aside. Put the egg yolks, 125 g (4½ oz/½ cup) of the sugar, lemon zest,
lemon juice and strained passionfruit juice in a heatproof bowl. Put the bowl over
a saucepan of simmering water and, using electric beaters, beat for 10 minutes, or
until thick and creamy. Remove from the heat and transfer to a glass bowl.

Sprinkle the gelatine over 125 ml (4 fl oz/½ cup) of water in a small bowl and
leave until spongy. Put the bowl in a pan of just-boiled water (the water should
come halfway up the bowl) and stir until dissolved. Add the gelatine to the
mousse mixture and mix well. Mix in the passionfruit pulp and leave until cold,
then fold in the whipped cream.

Using electric beaters, whisk the egg whites until soft peaks form. Gradually whisk
in the remaining sugar, beating until the sugar has dissolved. Fold the egg whites
into the mousse mixture quickly and lightly. Spoon into eight 250 ml (9 fl oz/
1 cup) ramekins or stemmed wine glasses. Refrigerate for 2 hours, or until set.
Sprinkle with the coconut just before serving

SERVES 10–12

Watermelon granita

450 g (1 lb) watermelon, skin and seeds removed
1 tablespoon liquid glucose or caster (superfine) sugar
½ teaspoon lemon juice

Purée the watermelon in a blender or food processor. Heat the glucose, lemon juice and 75 ml (2¼ fl oz) of water in a small saucepan for 4 minutes, or until dissolved. Add the watermelon and stir well.

Pour into a plastic freezer box, cover and freeze. Stir every 30 minutes with a fork during freezing to break up the ice crystals and give a better texture. Keep in the freezer until ready to serve, then roughly fork to break up the ice crystals.

SERVES 4

Chocolate and raspberry ice cream sandwich

300 g (10½ oz) frozen
   chocolate pound cake
2 tablespoons raspberry liqueur,
   optional
250 g (9 oz/2 cups) fresh or
   thawed raspberries

250 g (9 oz/1 cup) sugar
1 teaspoon lemon juice
1 litre (35 fl oz/4 cups) vanilla
   ice cream, softened
icing (confectioners') sugar,
   to dust

Using a sharp knife, cut the pound cake lengthwise into four thin slices. Using a 6.5 cm (2½ inch) plain cutter, cut eight rounds from the slices of cake. You will need two rounds of cake per person. Brush each round with half of the raspberry liqueur if using, then cover and set aside.

Line a 20 x 20 cm (8 x 8 inch) tin or dish with baking paper, leaving an overhang of paper on two opposite sides. Put the raspberries, sugar, lemon juice and remaining liqueur in a blender and blend to a smooth purée. Reserving 125 ml (4 fl oz/½ cup) of the purée, fold the remainder through the ice cream and pour into the tin. Freeze for 2 hours, or until firm.

Remove the ice cream from the freezer and use the overhanging baking paper to lift out. Using a 6.5 cm (2½ inch) cutter, cut four rounds from the ice cream.

To assemble, place four slices of cake on a tray, top each with a round of ice cream and then the remaining slices of cake. Smooth the sides of the ice cream to neaten, if necessary. Return the sandwiches to the freezer for 5 minutes to firm. Dust with icing sugar and serve with the remaining raspberry sauce.

SERVES 4

Cinnamon gelato

1 vanilla bean
550 ml (19 fl oz/2¼ cups) thick (double/heavy) cream
550 ml (19 fl oz/2¼ cups) milk
2 cinnamon sticks
6 egg yolks
100 g (3½ oz/½ cup) caster (superfine) sugar

Split the vanilla bean down the middle, leaving it joined at one end, and put it in a saucepan with the cream, milk and cinnamon sticks. Bring just to the boil, then remove from the heat and leave to infuse for 1 hour.

Whisk the egg yolks and sugar in a large bowl until pale and creamy. Pour the milk over the egg yolk mixture and whisk quickly to combine. Pour the custard back into the saucepan and cook over very low heat to just thicken it, stirring continuously with a wooden spoon. Remove from the heat and dip the spoon into the custard. Draw a line on the back of the spoon — if the line stays and the custard does not run through it, then it is ready; if not, cook a little longer. Do not allow the custard to boil.

Scrape out the vanilla seeds and mix them into the custard. Strain into a bowl, removing the vanilla bean and cinnamon sticks, and leave to cool. Churn in an ice-cream maker following the manufacturer's instructions. Or, pour into a metal or plastic freezer box and freeze, whisking every 30 minutes to break up the ice crystals and give a creamy texture. Once set, keep in the freezer until ready to serve.

SERVES 8

Mango fool

2 very ripe mangoes
250 ml (9 fl oz/1 cup) Greek-style yoghurt
4 tablespoons thick (double/heavy) cream

Remove the flesh off the mangoes. The easiest way to do this is to slice down either side of the stone so you have two 'cheeks'. Make crisscross cuts through the mango flesh on each cheek, almost through to the skin, then turn each cheek inside out and slice the flesh from the skin into a bowl. Cut the rest of the flesh from the stone.

Purée the flesh in a food processor or blender. Put 1 tablespoonful of mango purée in the bottom of four small glasses, bowls or cups. Top with a spoonful of yoghurt and then repeat. Spoon half the cream over each serving when you have used up all the mango and yoghurt. Swirl the layers together just before serving.

SERVES 4

Lemon frozen yoghurt

1 litre (35 fl oz/4 cups) low-fat vanilla yoghurt
185 ml (6 fl oz/¾ cup) lemon juice
185 g (6½ oz/¾ cup) caster (superfine) sugar
3 tablespoons light corn syrup
1 teaspoon finely grated lemon zest
½ teaspoon natural vanilla extract

Put the yoghurt in a fine sieve over a bowl and leave to drain in the refrigerator for at least 2 hours. Discard the liquid that drains off.

Put the remaining ingredients in a bowl and whisk together until the sugar dissolves. Add the drained yoghurt and whisk in well.

If you have an ice-cream machine, pour the mixture into it and churn according to the maker's instructions. Otherwise, place the mixture in a shallow metal tray and freeze for 2 hours, or until the mixture is frozen around the edges. Transfer to a large bowl and beat until smooth. Repeat this step three times. For the final freezing, place in an airtight container, cover the surface with a piece of greaseproof paper and a lid, and freeze for 4 hours or overnight. Serve in parfait glasses.

SERVES 6–8

Choc-dipped
ice cream balls

500 g (1 lb 2 oz) ice cream (use vanilla or a mixture of vanilla,
    pistachio and chocolate)
150 g (5½ oz) dark chocolate
150 g (5½ oz) white chocolate
150 g (5½ oz) milk chocolate
2 tablespoons toasted shelled walnuts, roughly chopped
2 tablespoons shelled pistachios, roughly chopped
2 tablespoons toasted shredded coconut

Line two large baking trays with baking paper and put in the freezer to chill.
Working quickly, use a melon baller to form 36 balls of ice cream and place on the
chilled baking trays. Place a cocktail stick in each ice cream ball. Return to the
freezer for 1 hour to freeze hard.

Place the chocolate in three separate heatproof bowls. Bring a saucepan of water
to the boil, then remove the pan from the heat. Sit one bowl at a time over the
pan, making sure the base of the bowl does not sit in the water. Stir occasionally
until the chocolate has melted. Remove the bowl from the heat and set aside to
cool; the chocolate should remain liquid; if it hardens, repeat.

Put the walnuts, pistachios and coconut in three separate small bowls. Working
with 12 of the ice cream balls, dip one at a time quickly in the dark chocolate, then
into the bowl with the walnuts. Return to the freezer. Repeat the process with
another 12 balls, dipping them in the melted white chocolate and the pistachios.
Dip the last 12 balls in the milk chocolate, then the toasted coconut. Freeze all the
ice cream balls for 1 hour.

MAKES 36

Caramel ice cream

70 g (2½ oz/⅓ cup) sugar
4 tablespoons thick (double/heavy) cream
3 egg yolks
360 ml (12 fl oz/1½ cups) milk
1 vanilla bean

To make the caramel, put 45 g (1½ oz) of the sugar in a heavy-based saucepan and heat until it dissolves and starts to caramelise — tip the saucepan from side to side as the sugar cooks to keep the colouring even. Remove from the heat and carefully add the cream (it will splutter). Stir over low heat until the caramel melts again.

Whisk the egg yolks and remaining sugar until light and fluffy. Put the milk and vanilla bean in a saucepan and bring just to the boil, then strain over the caramel. Bring back to the boil and pour over the egg yolk mixture, whisking continuously.

Pour the custard back into the pan and cook, stirring, until it is thick enough to coat the back of a wooden spoon. Do not let it boil or it will split. Pass through a sieve into a bowl and leave over ice to cool quickly.

Churn in an ice-cream maker following the manufacturer's instructions. Or, pour into a plastic freezer box, cover and freeze. Stir every 30 minutes with a whisk during freezing to break up the ice crystals. Freeze overnight with a layer of plastic wrap over the surface and the lid on the container. Keep in the freezer until ready to serve.

SERVES 4

Soy bavarois with mixed berries

2 egg yolks
60 g (2¼ oz/¼ cup) caster
(superfine) sugar
185 ml (6 fl oz/¾ cup) creamy
soy milk
1⅓ gelatine leaves
200 g (7 oz) berry tofu dessert,
lightly beaten

250 g (9 oz) mixed fresh or
frozen berries (such as
blackberries, strawberries,
raspberries, blueberries)
1 tablespoon caster (superfine)
sugar, extra

Lightly grease four 100 ml (3½ fl oz) metal dariole moulds.

Combine the egg yolks and sugar in a heatproof bowl. Heat the milk in a saucepan until almost boiling. Gradually pour onto the egg mixture, stirring. Put the bowl over a pan of simmering water, ensuring the bowl doesn't touch the water, and stir for 10 minutes, or until it thickens and coats the back of a spoon.

Soak the gelatine in cold water for 1 minute, or until softened. Squeeze any excess water from the gelatine, add to the egg mixture, stirring until dissolved. Place the bowl over iced water to chill, and whisk frequently. When cool, gently whisk in the tofu dessert until thoroughly combined. Pour into the moulds and refrigerate for at least 4 hours, or until set.

Put the mixed berries in a saucepan with the extra sugar. Cook, stirring, over low heat for 3–5 minutes, or until the sugar has dissolved. Leave to cool.

To serve, dip the dariole moulds in hot water for 3–5 seconds and turn out onto serving plates. Spoon the mixed berries and syrup around the bavarois and serve.

SERVES 4

Almond semifreddo

300 ml (10½ fl oz) thick (double/heavy) cream
4 eggs, at room temperature, separated
85 g (3 oz/⅔ cup) icing (confectioners') sugar
3 tablespoons Amaretto
80 g (2¾ oz/½ cup) blanched almonds, toasted and chopped
8 amaretti biscuits, crushed

fresh fruit or extra Amaretto

Whip the cream until firm peaks form, cover and chill. Line a 10 x 21 cm (4 x 8¼ inch) loaf (bar) tin with plastic wrap so that it overhangs the two long sides.

Place the egg yolks and icing sugar in a large bowl and beat until pale and creamy. Whisk the egg whites in a separate bowl until firm peaks form. Stir the Amaretto, almonds and amaretti biscuits into the egg yolk mixture, then carefully fold in the chilled cream and the egg whites until well combined. Carefully pour or spoon into the lined loaf tin and cover with the overhanging plastic. Freeze for 4 hours, or until frozen but not rock hard. Serve in slices with fresh fruit or a sprinkling of Amaretto. The semifreddo can also be poured into individual moulds or serving dishes before freezing.

SERVES 8–10

NOTE: Semifreddo means semi-frozen, so if you want to leave it in the freezer overnight, remove it and place it in the refrigerator for 30 minutes to soften slightly before serving.

Strawberry ice cream
with strawberry sauce

500 g (1 lb 2 oz) strawberries, hulled, washed and sliced
2 tablespoons caster (superfine) sugar
2 tablespoons Cointreau or fresh orange juice
500 ml (17 fl oz/2 cups) vanilla ice cream, slightly softened
125 g (4½ oz) blueberries (optional)

Put the strawberries in a small saucepan, add the sugar and Cointreau and cook over low heat for 5 minutes, or until softened and the juices are released. Remove from the heat and refrigerate.

Put half the strawberry mixture in a food processor or blender and process for 20–30 seconds, or until smooth. Spoon the ice cream into the food processor and process for 10 seconds, or until well combined with the strawberry mixture. Pour into a rectangular tin and return to the freezer for 2–3 hours, or until firm. Serve the ice cream with the reserved strawberry sauce and blueberries.

SERVES 4

NOTE: This ice cream is ready for the freezer in a very short time. You can freeze it overnight if you prefer.

Coffee gelato

5 egg yolks
115 g (4 oz/½ cup) sugar
500 ml (17 fl oz/2 cups) milk
125 ml (4 fl oz/½ cup) freshly made espresso coffee
1 tablespoon Tia Maria or coffee liqueur

Whisk the egg yolks and half the sugar in a bowl until you have a pale and creamy mixture. Pour the milk and coffee into a saucepan, add the remaining sugar and bring to the boil. Add to the egg mixture and whisk together. Pour back into the saucepan and cook over low heat, taking care that the custard doesn't boil. Stir constantly until the mixture is thick enough to coat the back of a wooden spoon. Strain the custard into a bowl and cool over ice before adding the Tia Maria.

To make the gelato by hand, pour the mixture into a freezerproof container, cover and freeze. Break up the ice crystals every 30 minutes with a fork to ensure a smooth texture. Repeat until it is ready — this may take 4 hours. If using an ice cream machine, follow the manufacturer's instructions.

SERVES 6

Coconut lime ice cream

25 g (1 oz/¼ cup) desiccated coconut
1½ tablespoons grated lime zest
4 tablespoons lime juice
4 tablespoons coconut milk powder
1 litre (35 fl oz/4 cups) good-quality vanilla ice cream, softened
coconut macaroon biscuits, to serve

Combine the desiccated coconut, grated lime zest, lime juice and coconut milk powder in a bowl and mix well.

Add the coconut mixture to the ice cream and fold through with a large metal spoon until evenly incorporated. Work quickly so that the ice cream does not melt. Return the mixture to the freezer and freeze for 30 minutes to firm. To serve, place 3 scoops in four latté glasses and serve with some coconut macaroon biscuits on the side.

SERVES 4

Eton mess

4–6 ready-made meringues
250 g (9 oz) strawberries, quartered
1 teaspoon caster (superfine) sugar
250 ml (9 fl oz/1 cup) pouring (whipping) cream

Break the meringues into pieces and set aside.

Put the strawberries in a bowl with the sugar. Using a potato masher or the back of a spoon, squash them slightly so they start to become juicy.

Whip the cream with a balloon or electric whisk until it is quite thick but not solid.

Mix everything together gently and spoon into glasses to serve.

SERVES 4

Choc-chip banana ice

600 ml (21 fl oz) ready-made low-fat custard
2 ripe bananas, mashed
2 teaspoons lemon juice
50 g (1¾ oz) dark chocolate

Combine the custard, mashed banana and lemon juice in a large mixing bowl. Beat using electric beaters until the banana and custard are well combined, with no lumps of banana remaining.

Pour into a metal cake tin, cover with plastic wrap and freeze for 3–4 hours, or until semi-frozen. Transfer to a chilled bowl and beat for 2 minutes using electric beaters until slushy, then return to the cake tin and put in the freezer for 2–3 hours, or until almost firm. Repeat the freezing and beating twice more (for a total of three times).

Finely chop the chocolate and fold into the mixture after the last beating. Refreeze in an airtight plastic container. Remove from the freezer and allow the ice cream to soften slightly before serving.

SERVES 6

Trifle

4 slices of Madeira (pound) cake or trifle sponges
3 tablespoons sweet sherry or Madeira
250 g (9 oz) raspberries
4 eggs
2 tablespoons caster (superfine) sugar
2 tablespoons plain (all-purpose) flour
500 ml (17 fl oz/2 cups) milk
¼ teaspoon natural vanilla extract
125 ml (4 fl oz/½ cup) pouring (whipping) cream, whipped
3 tablespoons flaked almonds, to decorate
raspberries, to decorate

Put the cake in the base of a serving bowl, then sprinkle it with the sherry. Scatter the raspberries over the top and crush them gently into the sponge with the back of a spoon to release their tart flavour, leaving some of them whole.

Mix the eggs, sugar and flour together in a bowl. Heat the milk in a saucepan. Pour over the egg mixture, stir well and pour back into a clean saucepan. Cook over medium heat until the custard boils and thickens and coats the back of a spoon. Stir in the vanilla, cover the surface with plastic wrap and leave to cool.

Pour the cooled custard over the raspberries and leave to set in the fridge — it will firm up but not become solid. Spoon the whipped cream over the custard. Decorate with almonds and raspberries and refrigerate until needed.

SERVES 6

Raspberry mousse

300 g (10½ oz) fresh or thawed frozen raspberries
400 g (14 oz) vanilla fromage frais or whipped yoghurt
1 tablespoon gelatine
2 egg whites
2 tablespoons sugar
raspberries, extra, to garnish

Mash the raspberries roughly with a fork. Combine in a large bowl with the fromage frais.

Put 2 tablespoons of hot water in a small heatproof bowl and sprinkle with the gelatine. Stand the bowl in a saucepan of very hot water, and stir until the gelatine has dissolved and the mixture is smooth. Cool slightly, then whisk through the raspberry mixture.

Using electric beaters, beat the egg whites in a dry bowl until soft peaks form. Add the sugar, 1 tablespoon at a time, beating until dissolved. Gently fold through the berry mixture. Spoon into eight 150 ml (5 fl oz) moulds, and refrigerate for 2 hours, or until set. Turn out onto a plate and serve with the extra raspberries.

SERVES 8

baked

Apple crumble

8 apples
90 g (3¼ oz/⅓ cup) caster (superfine) sugar
zest of 1 lemon
120 g (4 oz) butter
125 g (4½ oz/1 cup) plain (all-purpose) flour
1 teaspoon ground cinnamon
thick (double/heavy) cream, to serve

Preheat the oven to 180°C (350°/Gas 4). Peel and core the apples, then cut into chunks. Put the apple, 2 tablespoons of the sugar and the lemon zest in a small baking dish and mix together. Dot 40 g (1½ oz) of butter over the top.

Rub the remaining butter into the flour until the mixture resembles coarse breadcrumbs. Stir in the rest of the sugar and the cinnamon. Add 1–2 tablespoons of water and stir the crumbs together so they form bigger clumps.

Sprinkle the crumble mixture over the apple and bake the crumble for 1 hour 15 minutes, or until the top should be browned and the juice is bubbling up through the crumble. Serve with cream.

SERVES 4

Cherry pie

500 g (1 lb 2 oz) ready-made sweet shortcrust pastry
850 g (1 lb 14 oz) tinned seedless black cherries, drained well
60 g (2¼ oz/⅓ cup) soft brown sugar
1½ teaspoons ground cinnamon
1 teaspoon finely grated lemon zest
1 teaspoon finely grated orange zest
1–2 drops almond extract
25 g (1 oz/¼ cup) ground almonds
1 egg, lightly beaten

Preheat the oven to 190°C (375°F/Gas 5). Roll out two-thirds of the dough between two sheets of baking paper to form a circle large enough to fit a 22 x 20 x 2 cm (8½ x 8 x ¾ inch) pie plate. Remove the top sheet of baking paper and invert the pastry into the pie plate. Cut away the excess pastry with a small sharp knife. Roll out the remaining pastry large enough to cover the pie. Refrigerate, covered in plastic wrap, for 20 minutes.

Put the cherries, sugar, cinnamon, lemon and orange zests, and almond extract in a bowl and mix to coat the cherries.

Line the pastry base with the ground almonds. Spoon in the filling, brush the pastry edges with beaten egg, and cover with the pastry lid. Use a fork to seal the edges pastry. Cut four slits in the top of the pie to allow steam to escape, then brush the pastry with beaten egg. Bake for 1 hour, or until the pastry is golden and the juices are bubbling through the slits in the pastry. Serve warm.

SERVES 6

Mango and passionfruit pies

750 g (1 lb 10 oz) ready-made sweet shortcrust pastry
3 ripe mangoes, peeled and sliced or chopped,
    or 400 g (14 oz) tinned mango slices, drained
60 g (2¼ oz/¼ cup) passionfruit pulp, strained
1 tablespoon custard powder
90 g (3¼ oz/⅓ cup) caster (superfine) sugar
1 egg, lightly beaten
icing (confectioners') sugar, to dust

Preheat the oven to 190°C (375°F/Gas 5). Grease six 10 x 8 x 3 cm (4 x 3¼ x 1¼ inch) fluted flan tins or round pie dishes. Roll out two-thirds of the pastry between two sheets of baking paper to a thickness of 3 mm (⅛ inch). Cut out six 13 cm (5 inch) circles. Line the tins with the circles and trim the edges. Refrigerate while you make the filling.

Combine the mango, passionfruit, custard powder and sugar in a bowl.

Roll out the remaining pastry between two sheets of baking paper to 3 mm (⅛ inch) thick. Cut out six 11 cm (4¼ inch) circles. Re-roll the pastry trimmings and cut into shapes for decoration.

Fill the pastry cases with the mango mixture and brush the edges with egg. Top with the pastry circles and press the edges to seal. Trim the edges and decorate with the pastry shapes. Brush the tops with beaten egg and dust with icing sugar.

Bake for 20–25 minutes, or until the pastry is golden brown. Served with cream.

MAKES 6

Lemon delicious

70 g (2½ oz) unsalted butter, at room temperature
185 g (6½ oz/¾ cup) sugar
2 teaspoons finely grated lemon zest
3 eggs, separated
30 g (1 oz/¼ cup) self-raising flour
185 ml (6 fl oz/¾ cup) milk
4 tablespoons lemon juice
icing (confectioners') sugar, to dust
thick (double/heavy) cream, to serve

Preheat the oven to 180°C (350°F/Gas 4). Melt 10 g (¼ oz) of the butter and use to lightly grease a 1.25 litre (44 fl oz/5 cup) ovenproof ceramic dish.

Using electric beaters, beat the remaining butter, the sugar and grated zest together in a bowl until light and creamy. Gradually add the egg yolks, beating well after each addition. Fold in the flour and milk alternately to make a smooth but runny batter. Stir in the lemon juice.

Whisk the egg whites in a dry bowl until firm peaks form and, with a large metal spoon, fold a third of the whites into the batter. Gently fold in the remaining egg whites, being careful not to overmix.

Pour the batter into the prepared dish and place in a large roasting tin. Pour enough hot water into the tin to come one-third of the way up the side of the dish. Bake for 55 minutes, or until the top of the pudding is golden, risen and firm to the touch. Leave for 5 minutes before serving. Dust with icing sugar and serve with cream.

SERVES 4–6

Freeform blueberry pie

Pastry
185 g (6½ oz/1½ cups) plain
 (all-purpose) flour
100 g (3½ oz) unsalted butter,
 chilled and cubed
2 teaspoons grated orange zest
1 tablespoon caster (superfine)
 sugar
2–3 tablespoons iced water

40 g (1½ oz/⅓ cup) crushed
 amaretti biscuits
60 g (2¼ oz/½ cup) plain
 (all-purpose) flour
1 teaspoon ground cinnamon
90 g (3¼ oz/⅓ cup) caster
 (superfine) sugar
500 g (1 lb 2 oz) blueberries
milk, for brushing
2 tablespoons blueberry jam
icing (confectioners') sugar,
 to dust

Sift the flour into a bowl and rub in the butter until the mixture resembles breadcrumbs. Stir in the orange zest and sugar. Make a well, add almost all the water and mix with a flat-bladed knife, using a cutting action, until the mixture comes together in beads. Add a little more water if necessary. Gather together and lift out onto a lightly floured surface. Press together into a ball and flatten it slightly into a disc. Cover in plastic wrap and refrigerate for 20 minutes.

Preheat the oven to 200°C (400°F/Gas 6). Combine the biscuits, flour, cinnamon and 1½ tablespoons of the sugar. Roll the pastry out to a 36 cm (14¼ inch) circle and sprinkle with the biscuit mixture, leaving a 4 cm (1½ inch) border. Arrange the blueberries over the biscuits, then bring up the edges to form a freeform crust.

Brush the sides of the pie with the milk. Sprinkle with the remaining sugar and bake for 30 minutes, or until the sides are crisp and brown. Warm the jam in a saucepan over low heat and brush over the berries. Cool to room temperature, then dust the pastry crust with sifted icing sugar.

SERVES 6–8

Passionfruit soufflé

caster (superfine) sugar, for lining
40 g (1½ oz) unsalted butter
2 tablespoons plain (all-purpose) flour
185 ml (6 fl oz/¾ cup) milk
125 g (4½ oz/½ cup) caster (superfine) sugar
250 ml (9 fl oz/1 cup) fresh passionfruit pulp
    (about 7 large passionfruit)
6 egg whites
icing (confectioners') sugar, to dust

Preheat the oven to 180°C (350°F/Gas 4). Put a baking tray in the oven to heat. Lightly grease four 300 ml (10½ fl oz) ovenproof ramekins with oil and sprinkle the base and side with caster sugar, shaking out any excess.

Melt the butter in a saucepan over medium heat, add the flour and stir for 1 minute, or until foaming. Remove from the heat and gradually add the milk. Return to the heat and stir constantly for 5–6 minutes, or until the sauce boils and thickens. Reduce the heat and simmer, stirring, for 2 minutes. Transfer to a bowl and stir in the sugar and passionfruit pulp. Do not worry if the mixture looks curdled.

Using electric beaters, beat the egg whites in a dry bowl until firm peaks form. Using a metal spoon, fold a large dollop of the beaten egg white into the passionfruit mixture, then gently fold in the remaining egg white. Spoon the mixture into the ramekins. Place on the baking tray and bake for 18–20 minutes, or until golden and well risen but still a bit wobbly. Dust with icing sugar and serve immediately.

SERVES 4

Raisin pie

600 g (1 lb 5 oz) ready-made
  sweet shortcrust pastry
4 tablespoons orange juice
2 tablespoons lemon juice
320 g (11¼ oz/2½ cups) raisins
140 g (5 oz/¾ cup) soft brown
  sugar
½ teaspoon mixed spice

30 g (1 oz/¼ cup) cornflour
  (cornstarch)
1 teaspoon finely grated lemon
  zest
1 teaspoon finely grated
  orange zest
1 egg, lightly beaten
1 tablespoon sugar, to sprinkle

Preheat the oven to 190°C (375°F/Gas 5). Put a baking tray in the oven to heat.. Grease a 23 x 18 x 3 cm (9 x 7 x 1¼ inch) pie tin. Roll out two-thirds of the pastry between two sheets of baking paper to fit the base and side of the dish. Remove the top paper and invert the pastry into the tin, pressing it into the tin. Trim the excess. Chill the base and remaining pastry.

Combine the citrus juices, raisins and 250 ml (9 fl oz/1 cup) of water in a saucepan. Boil over high heat, stirring occasionally, for 2 minutes. Remove from the heat.

Mix the brown sugar, mixed spice and cornflour in a bowl. Add 125 ml (4 fl oz/ ½ cup) of water and mix until smooth. Slowly stir into the raisin mixture and return the pan to the stove over high heat. Boil, stirring, then reduce to a simmer, stirring occasionally, for 5 minutes, or until it thickens. Stir in the citrus zest and cool for 30 minutes.

Roll out the remaining pastry to cover the pie. Fill the base with the raisin mixture, brush the edges with the egg and cover with the pastry top. Pinch the edges together and make a few small holes. Brush with egg, sprinkle with sugar and bake for 40 minutes, or until golden. Serve warm or cold.

SERVES 6–8

Peach pie

500 g (1 lb 2 oz) ready-made sweet shortcrust pastry
1.65 kg (3 lb 8 oz) tinned peach slices, well-drained
125 g (4½ oz/½ cup) caster (superfine) sugar
30 g (1 oz/¼ cup) cornflour (cornstarch)
¼ teaspoon almond extract
20 g (¾ oz) unsalted butter, chopped
1 tablespoon milk
1 egg, lightly beaten
caster (superfine) sugar, to sprinkle

Roll out two-thirds of the dough between two sheets of baking paper until large enough to line a 23 x 18 x 3 cm (9 x 7 x 1¼ inch) pie tin. Remove the top sheet of paper and invert the pastry into the tin. Use a small ball of pastry to press the pastry into the tin. Trim any excess pastry with a knife. Refrigerate for 20 minutes.

Preheat the oven to 200°C (400°F/Gas 6). Line the pastry with crumpled baking paper and pour in baking beads or rice. Bake for 10 minutes, remove the paper and beads and return to the oven for 5 minutes, or until the pastry base is dry and lightly coloured. Allow to cool.

Mix the peaches, sugar, cornflour and almond essence in a bowl, then spoon into the pastry shell. Dot with butter and moisten the edges with milk.

Roll out the remaining dough to a 25 cm (10 inch) square. Using a fluted pastry cutter, cut into ten strips 2.5 cm (1 inch) wide. Lay the strips in a lattice pattern over the filling, pressing firmly on the edges and trim. Brush with egg and sprinkle with sugar. Bake for 10 minutes, reduce the heat to 180°C (350°F/Gas 4) and bake for 30 minutes, or until golden. Cool before serving.

SERVES 6

Pear and almond flan

155 g (5½ oz/1¼ cups) plain
(all-purpose) flour
90 g (3¼ oz) unsalted butter,
chilled and chopped
60 g (2¼ oz/¼ cup) caster
(superfine) sugar
2 egg yolks

Filling
165 g (5¾ oz) unsalted butter
160 g (5½ oz/⅔ cup) caster
(superfine) sugar
3 eggs
230 g (8 oz/2¼ cups) ground
almonds
1½ tablespoons plain
(all-purpose) flour
2 ripe pears, peeled, halved
lengthways, cores removed

Grease a shallow 24 cm (9½ inch) round flan tin with a removable base. Put the flour, butter and caster sugar in a food processor and process until the mixture resembles breadcrumbs. Add the egg yolks and about 1 tablespoon of water until the mixture just comes together. Turn out onto a floured surface and gather into a ball. Cover in plastic wrap and refrigerate for 30 minutes. Preheat the oven to 180°C (350°F/Gas 4).

Roll the pastry between baking paper dusted with flour and line the tin with the pastry. Trim off any excess. Prick the base a few times. Blind bake the pastry for 10 minutes. Remove the paper and beads and bake for 10 minutes.

To make the filling, mix the butter and sugar with electric beaters for 30 seconds only. Add the eggs one at a time, beating after each addition. Fold in the ground almonds and flour and spread the filling over the cooled base. Cut the pears crossways into 3 mm slices, separate them slightly, then place on top of the tart to form a cross. Bake for 50 minutes, or until the filling has set (the middle may still be a little soft). Cool in the tin, then refrigerate for 2 hours before serving.

SERVES 8

Rhubarb and berry crumble

850 g (1 lb 14 oz) rhubarb, cut into 2.5 cm (1 inch) lengths
150 g (5½ oz/1¼ cups) blackberries
1 teaspoon grated orange zest
250 g (9 oz/1 cup) caster (superfine) sugar
125 g (4½ oz/1 cup) plain (all-purpose) flour
115 g (4 oz/1 cup) ground almonds
½ teaspoon ground ginger
150 g (5½ oz) chilled unsalted butter, cubed

Preheat the oven to 180°C (350°F/Gas 4). Lightly grease a deep 1.5 litre (52 fl oz/ 6 cup) ovenproof dish.

Bring a saucepan of water to the boil over high heat, add the rhubarb, and cook for 2 minutes, or until just tender. Drain well and combine with the berries, orange zest and 90 g (3¼ oz/⅓ cup) of the caster sugar. Add a little more sugar if needed. Spoon the fruit mixture into the prepared dish.

To make the topping, combine the flour, ground almonds, ginger and the remaining sugar. Rub the butter into the flour mixture until it resembles coarse breadcrumbs. Sprinkle the crumble mix over the fruit, pressing lightly.

Put the dish on a baking tray and bake for 25–30 minutes, or until the topping is golden and the fruit is bubbling underneath. Leave for 5 minutes, then serve with cream or ice cream.

SERVES 4

NOTE: Substitute raspberries, loganberries or blueberries for the blackberries. Strawberries do not work well as they become too soft when cooked.

Nutty fig pie

375 g (13 oz) ready-made
   shortcrust pastry
200 g (7 oz/1½ cups) hazelnuts
100 g (3½ oz/⅔ cup) pine nuts
100 g (3½ oz/1 cup) flaked
   almonds
100 g (3½ oz/⅔ cup) blanched
   almonds

170 ml (5½ fl oz/⅔ cup)
   pouring (whipping) cream
60 g (2¼ oz) unsalted butter
90 g (3¼ oz/¼ cup) honey
95 g (3¼ oz) soft brown sugar
150 g (5½ oz) dessert figs, cut
   into quarters
chocolate ice cream, to serve

Preheat the oven to 200°C (400°F/Gas 6). Grease a 23 x 18 x 3 cm (9 x 7 x 1¼ inch) pie tin. Roll the pastry out between two sheets of baking paper until large enough to cover the base and side of the pie tin. Remove the top sheet and invert the pastry into the tin, allowing any excess to hang over. Trim with a knife and prick the base several times with a fork. Score the edge with a fork. Refrigerate for 20 minutes, then bake for 15 minutes, or until lightly golden. Allow to cool.

Bake the hazelnuts on a baking tray for 8 minutes, or until the skins start to peel away. Tip into a tea towel (dish towel) and rub to remove the skins. Put the pine nuts, flaked almonds and blanched almonds on a baking tray and bake for 5–6 minutes, or until lightly golden.

Put the cream, butter, honey and brown sugar in a saucepan over medium heat. Stir until the sugar dissolves and the butter melts. Remove from the heat and stir in the nuts and figs. Spoon the mixture into the pastry case and bake for 30 minutes. Remove and cool until firm before slicing. Served with chocolate ice cream.

SERVES 8

Plum cobbler

825 g (1 lb 13 oz) tinned dark
   plums, pitted
1 tablespoon honey
2 ripe pears, peeled, cored and
   cut into eighths

Topping
250 g (9 oz/1 cup) self-raising
   flour
1 tablespoon caster (superfine)
   sugar

¼ teaspoon ground cardamom
   or ground cinnamon
40 g (1½ oz) unsalted butter,
   chilled and chopped
3 tablespoons milk, plus extra,
   for brushing
1 tablespoon caster (superfine)
   sugar, extra
¼ teaspoon ground cardamom
   or ground cinnamon, extra

Preheat the oven to 200°C (400°F/Gas 6). Grease an 18 cm (7 inch) round
ovenproof dish. Drain the plums, reserving 185 ml (6 fl oz/¾ cup) of the syrup.
Put the syrup, honey and pear in a large saucepan and bring to the boil. Reduce
the heat and simmer for 8 minutes, or until the pear is tender. Add the plums.

To make the topping, sift the flour, sugar, cardamom and a pinch of salt into a
bowl. Rub in the butter until it resembles fine breadcrumbs. Stir in the milk using
a flat-bladed knife, mixing lightly to form a soft dough — add a little more milk if
necessary. Turn onto a lightly floured surface and form into a smooth ball. Roll
out to a 1 cm thickness and cut into rounds with a 4 cm cutter.

Spoon the hot fruit into the dish, then arrange the circles of dough in an overlapping
pattern over the fruit, on the inside edge of the dish only — leave the fruit in the
centre exposed. Brush the dough with the extra milk. Mix the extra sugar and
cardamom and sprinkle over the dough. Put the dish on a baking tray and bake for
30 minutes, or until the topping is golden and cooked.

SERVES 4

Apple sago pudding

90 g (3¼ oz/⅓ cup) caster (superfine) sugar
100 g (3½ oz/½ cup) sago
600 ml (21 fl oz/2½ cups) milk
55 g (2 oz/½ cup) sultanas
1 teaspoon natural vanilla extract
pinch ground nutmeg
¼ teaspoon ground cinnamon
2 eggs, lightly beaten
3 small ripe apples, peeled, cored and very thinly sliced
1 tablespoon soft brown sugar

Preheat the oven to 180°C (350°F/Gas 4). Grease a 1.5 litre (52 fl oz/6 cup) ceramic soufflé dish.

Put the sugar, sago, milk, sultanas and ¼ teaspoon salt in a saucepan over medium heat. Cook, stirring often. Bring to the boil, then reduce the heat and simmer for 5 minutes.

Stir in the vanilla extract, nutmeg, cinnamon, egg and the apple slices. Pour into the prepared dish and sprinkle with the brown sugar. Bake for 45 minutes, or until set and golden brown.

SERVES 4

Rhubarb pie

Pastry

250 g (9 oz/2 cups) plain (all-purpose) flour

30 g (1 oz) unsalted butter, cubed

70 g (2½ oz) copha (white vegetable shortening)

2 tablespoons icing (confectioners') sugar

160 ml (5¼ fl oz/⅔ cup) iced water

1.5 kg (3 lb 5 oz) rhubarb, cut into 2 cm (¾ inch) pieces

250 g (9 oz/1 cup) caster (superfine) sugar

½ teaspoon ground cinnamon

2½ tablespoons cornflour (cornstarch), with 3 tablespoons water

30 g (1 oz) unsalted butter

1 egg, lightly beaten

icing (confectioners') sugar, to dust

Grease a 25 x 20 x 4 cm (10 x 8 x 1½ inch) ceramic pie dish. Sift the flour and ½ teaspoon salt into a bowl and rub in the butter and copha until the mixture resembles breadcrumbs. Stir in the icing sugar. Make a well, add most of the water and mix with a knife, using a cutting action, until it comes together in beads. Add more water if needed. Gather the dough and put on a floured surface. Press into a ball, flatten a little and cover in plastic wrap. Refrigerate for 30 minutes.

Put the rhubarb, sugar, cinnamon and 2 tablespoons of water in a saucepan over low heat. Stir until the sugar dissolves. Simmer, covered, for 5–8 minutes, or until the rhubarb is tender. Add the cornflour and water mixture. Bring to the boil, stirring. Cool. Preheat the oven to 180°C (350°F/Gas 4) and heat a baking tray.

Roll out two-thirds of the dough to a 30 cm (12 inch) circle and put into the pie dish. Spoon in the rhubarb and dot with butter. Roll out the remaining pastry for a lid. Brush the pie rim with egg and press the top in place. Trim the edges and make a slit in the top. Decorate with pastry scraps and brush with egg. Bake on the hot tray for 35 minutes, or until golden. Dust with icing sugar.

SERVES 6

Lime and blueberry pie

375 g (13 oz) ready-made sweet shortcrust pastry
3 eggs
125 g (4½ oz/½ cup) caster (superfine) sugar
3 tablespoons buttermilk
1 tablespoon lime juice
2 teaspoons grated lime zest
2 tablespoons custard powder
250 g (9 oz/1⅔ cups) blueberries
icing (confectioners') sugar, to dust

Roll out the pastry between two sheets of baking paper to line a 23 x 18 x 3 cm (9 x 7 x 1¼ inch) pie tin. Remove the top paper and invert the pastry into the tin. Use a small ball of pastry to press the pastry into the tin. Trim any excess pastry. Refrigerate for 20 minutes.

Preheat the oven to 200°C (400°F/Gas 6). Line the base and side of the pastry with crumpled baking paper and pour in baking beads or rice. Bake for 10 minutes, remove the paper and beads and bake for 4–5 minutes, or until the base is dry and lightly coloured. Cool slightly. Reduce the oven to 180°C (350°F/Gas 4).

To make the filling, beat the eggs and caster sugar in a bowl using electric beaters until the mixture is thick and pale. Add the buttermilk, lime juice, zest and sifted custard powder. Stir until combined, then spoon into the pastry shell. Bake for 15 minutes, then reduce the temperature to 160°C (315°F/Gas 2–3) and cook for another 20–25 minutes, or until the filling has coloured slightly and is set. Cool, then top with the blueberries. Dust with sifted icing sugar and serve.

SERVES 6–8

Baked custards

10 g (¼ oz) unsalted butter, melted
3 eggs
90 g (3¼ oz/⅓ cup) caster (superfine) sugar
500 ml (17 fl oz/2 cups) milk
125 ml (4 fl oz/½ cup) pouring (whipping) cream
1½ teaspoons vanilla extract
ground nutmeg

Preheat the oven to 160°C (315°F/Gas 2–3). Brush four 250 ml (9 fl oz/1 cup) ramekins or a 1.5 litre (52 fl oz/6 cup) ovenproof dish with the melted butter.

Whisk together the eggs and sugar in a large bowl until they are combined. Put the milk and cream in a small saucepan over medium heat. Stir for 3–4 minutes, or until the mixture is warmed through, then stir into the egg mixture with the vanilla essence. Strain into the prepared dishes and sprinkle with the ground nutmeg.

Put the dishes in a deep roasting tin and add enough hot water to come halfway up the side of the dishes. Bake for 25 minutes for the individual custards, or 30 minutes for the large custard, or until it is set and a knife inserted into the centre comes out clean.

Remove the custards from the roasting tin and leave for 10 minutes before serving.

SERVES 4

Lemon meringue pie

375 g (13 oz) ready-made sweet shortcrust pastry
30 g (1 oz/¼ cup) plain (all-purpose) flour
30 g (1 oz/¼ cup) cornflour (cornstarch)
250 g (9 oz/1 cup) caster (superfine) sugar
185 ml (6 fl oz/¾ cup) lemon juice
1 tablespoon grated lemon zest
50 g (1¾ oz) unsalted butter, chopped
6 egg yolks

Meringue
6 egg whites
pinch cream of tartar
340 g (11¾ oz) caster (superfine) sugar

Grease a 25 x 18 x 3 cm (10 x 7 x 1¼ inch) pie plate. Roll the pastry out between two sheets of baking paper into a 30 cm (12 inch) circle. Invert the pastry into the plate. Trim the edges. Re-roll pastry trimmings and cut into strips. Brush the pie rim with water, place the strips around the top and make a decorative edge. Prick over the base with a fork. Cover and refrigerate for 20 minutes. Preheat the oven to 180°C (350°F/Gas 4). Blind bake the pastry for 15 minutes. Remove the beads and bake for 15–20 minutes. Cool. Increase the oven to 200°C (400°F/Gas 6). Put the flours, sugar, lemon juice and zest in a saucepan. Add 315 ml (10¾ fl oz/1¼ cups) of water and whisk over until smooth. Cook, stirring, for 2 minutes, or until thick. Remove from the heat and whisk in the butter and egg yolks. Return to low heat and stir, for 2 minutes.

To make the meringue, beat the egg whites and cream of tartar until soft peaks form. Pour in the caster sugar, beating until thick and glossy. Spread the lemon filling into the pastry base, then cover with the meringue, piling high in the centre and making peaks with a knife. Bake for 8–10 minutes, or until lightly browned.

SERVES 4–6

Key lime pie

375 g (13 oz) ready-made sweet shortcrust pastry
4 egg yolks
395 g (13¾ oz) tinned condensed milk
125 ml (4 fl oz/½ cup) lime juice
2 teaspoons grated lime zest
lime slices, to garnish
icing (confectioners') sugar, to dust
whipped cream, to serve

Preheat the oven to 180°C (350°F/Gas 4). Grease a 23 cm (9 inch) loose-bottomed flan tin. Roll the dough out between two sheets of baking paper until it is large enough to fit into the pie tin. Remove the top sheet of paper and invert the pastry into the tin. Use a small ball of pastry to help press the pastry into the tin, allowing any excess to hang over the sides. Use a sharp knife to trim away any extra pastry.

Line the pastry shell with a piece of crumpled baking paper that is large enough to cover the base and side of the tin and pour in some baking beads or rice. Bake for 10 minutes, remove the paper and beads and return the pastry to the oven for a further 4–5 minutes, or until the base is dry. Leave to cool.

Using electric beaters, beat the egg yolks, condensed milk, lime juice and zest in a large bowl for 2 minutes, or until well combined. Pour into the pie shell and smooth the surface. Bake for 20–25 minutes, or until set. Allow the pie to cool, then refrigerate for 2 hours, or until well chilled. Garnish with lime slices, dust with sifted icing sugar and serve with whipped cream.

SERVES 6–8

Blackberry pie

500 g (1 lb 2 oz) ready-made sweet shortcrust pastry
500 g (1 lb 2 oz/4 cups) blackberries
160 g (5¾ oz/⅔ cup) caster (superfine) sugar
2 tablespoons cornflour (cornstarch)
milk, to brush
1 egg, lightly beaten
caster (superfine) sugar, extra, to sprinkle

Preheat the oven to 200°C (400°F/Gas 6). Grease a 26 x 20.5 x 4.5 cm (10½ x 8 x 1¾ inch) ceramic pie dish. Roll out two-thirds of the pastry between two sheets of baking paper until large enough to line the base and side of the pie dish. Remove the top paper, invert the pastry into the dish and press firmly into place, leaving the excess overhanging the edges.

Toss the blackberries (if frozen, thaw and drain well), sugar and cornflour together in a bowl until well mixed, then transfer to the pie dish. Roll out the remaining pastry between two sheets of baking paper until large enough to cover the pie. Moisten the rim of the pie base with milk and press the pastry lid firmly into place. Trim and crimp the edges. Brush with egg and sprinkle with the extra sugar. Pierce the top of the pie with a knife.

Bake on the bottom shelf of the oven for 10 minutes. Reduce the oven to 180°C (350°F/Gas 4) and move the pie to the centre shelf. Bake for a further 30 minutes, or until golden on top. Cool before serving with cream or ice cream.

SERVES 6

Apricot honey soufflé

180 g (6½ oz/1 cup) dried whole apricots, chopped
2 tablespoons caster (superfine) sugar
2 egg yolks
1½ tablespoons honey, warmed
1 teaspoon finely grated lemon zest
4 egg whites
icing (confectioners') sugar, to dust

Place the apricots in a saucepan with 125 ml (4 fl oz/½ cup) of cold water. Bring to the boil, then reduce the heat and simmer for 20 minutes, or until the apricots are soft and pulpy. Drain, then process in a food processor to a purée.

Preheat the oven to 200°C (400°F/Gas 6). Lightly grease a 1.25 litre (44 fl oz/5 cup) soufflé dish and sprinkle the base and side with 1 tablespoon of caster sugar. Put the egg yolks, honey, zest and apricot purée in a bowl and beat until smooth.

Whisk the egg whites in a dry bowl until soft peaks form, then whisk in the remaining sugar. Fold 1 tablespoon into the apricot mixture and mix well. Lightly fold in the remaining egg white, being careful to keep the mixture light and aerated. Spoon into the soufflé dish and level the surface. Run your thumb around the inside rim to create a gap between the mixture and the wall of the dish (this will encourage even rising).

Bake on the upper shelf in the oven for 25–30 minutes, or until risen and just set. Cover loosely with foil if the surface starts to overbrown. Dust with icing sugar and serve.

SERVES 4

Tarte au citron

Pastry
350 g (12 oz/2¾ cups) plain
(all-purpose) flour
150 g (5½ oz) unsalted butter
100 g (3½ oz/¾ cup) icing sugar
2 eggs, beaten

Filing
2 eggs

2 egg yolks
275 g (9¾ oz/1¼ cups) caster
(superfine) sugar
200 ml (7 fl oz) thick
(double/heavy) cream
250 ml (9 fl oz/1 cup) lemon
juice
finely grated zest of 3 lemons

To make the pastry, sift the flour and salt onto a work surface and make a well. Put the butter into the well and work, using a pecking action with your fingertips and thumb, until it is very soft. Add the sugar to the butter and mix. Add the eggs to the butter and mix. Gradually incorporate the flour. Bring together, knead a few times to make a smooth dough, then roll into a ball. Cover in plastic wrap and refrigerate for at least 1 hour.

Preheat the oven to 190°C (375 F/Gas 5). Roll out the pastry to line a 23 cm (9 inch) round loose-based fluted tart tin. Chill for 20 minutes. To make the filling, whisk together the eggs, egg yolks and sugar. Add the cream, whisking all the time, then the lemon juice and zest.

Blind bake the pastry for 10 minutes, remove the paper and bake for 3–5 minutes, or until the pastry is just cooked. Remove from the oven and reduce the oven to 150°C (300 F/Gas 2). Put the tin on a baking tray and carefully pour the filling into the pastry case. Return to the oven for 35-40 minutes, or until set. Cool before serving.

SERVES 6

Old-fashioned
apple pie

Pastry

250 g (9 oz/2 cups) self-raising
flour

85 g (3 oz/⅔ cup) cornflour
(cornstarch)

180 g (6½ oz) unsalted butter,
chilled and cubed

90 g (3¼ oz/⅓ cup) caster
(superfine) sugar

1 egg, lightly beaten

40 g (1½ oz) unsalted butter

6 green apples, peeled, cored
and thinly sliced

1 tablespoon lemon juice

140 g (5 oz/¾ cup) soft brown
sugar, plus extra to sprinkle

1 teaspoon ground nutmeg

2 tablespoons plain (all-
purpose) flour with
3 tablespoons water

25 g (1 oz) ground almonds

milk, to brush

Grease a 1 litre (35 fl oz/4 cup) metal pie dish. Sift the flours into a bowl and rub
in the butter. Stir in the sugar and a pinch of salt. Make a well, add the egg and
mix. Press the dough into a smooth disc, cover with plastic wrap and refrigerate
for 20 minutes. Use two-thirds of the dough to line the base and side of the dish.
Roll out the remaining dough to make a lid. Cover and refrigerate for 20 minutes.
Preheat the oven to 200°C (400°F/Gas 6) and heat a baking tray.

Melt the butter in a frying pan, add the apple and toss. Stir in the lemon juice,
sugar and nutmeg and cook for 10 minutes. Add the flour and water mixture, then
the almonds. Bring to the boil and cook, stirring, for 2–3 minutes. Pour into a
bowl and cool. Put the apple in the pastry case. Cover with the pastry lid and
press onto the rim. Trim the edges and pinch together. Prick over the top, brush
with milk and sprinkle with sugar. Bake for 40 minutes, or until golden.

SERVES 8

Cherry clafoutis

500 g (1 lb 2 oz) cherries
90 g (3¼ oz/¾ cup) plain (all-purpose) flour
2 eggs, lightly beaten
90 g (3¼ oz/⅓ cup) caster (superfine) sugar
250 ml (9 fl oz/1 cup) milk
3 tablespoons thick (double/heavy) cream
50 g (1¾ oz) unsalted butter, melted
icing (confectioners') sugar, to dust

Preheat the oven to 180°C (350°F/Gas 4). Lightly brush a 1.5 litre (52 fl oz/6 cup) ovenproof dish with melted butter.

Carefully pit the cherries, then spread into the dish in a single layer.

Sift the flour into a bowl, add the egg and whisk until smooth. Add the caster sugar, milk, cream and butter, whisking until just combined, but being careful not to overbeat.

Pour the batter over the cherries and bake for 30–40 minutes, or until a skewer comes out clean when inserted into the centre. Remove from the oven and dust generously with icing sugar. Serve immediately.

SERVES 6–8

Amaretti-stuffed peaches

6 ripe peaches
60 g (2¼ oz) amaretti biscuits, crushed
1 egg yolk
2 tablespoons caster (superfine) sugar
20 g (¾ oz/¼ cup) ground almonds
1 tablespoon amaretto
3 tablespoons white wine
1 teaspoon caster (superfine) sugar, extra
20 g (¾ oz) unsalted butter

Preheat the oven to 180°C (350°F/Gas 4). Lightly grease a 30 x 25 cm (10 x 8 inch) ovenproof dish with butter.

Cut each peach in half and carefully remove the stones. Scoop a little of the pulp out from each and combine in a small bowl with the crushed biscuits, egg yolk, caster sugar, ground almonds and amaretto.

Spoon some of the mixture into each peach and place cut side up in the dish. Sprinkle with the white wine and the extra sugar. Put a dot of butter on the top of each and bake for 20–25 minutes, or until golden.

SERVES 6

Bread and butter pudding

50 g (1¾ oz) unsalted butter
8 thick slices day-old white bread
1 teaspoon ground cinnamon
2 tablespoons sultanas
3 eggs
1 egg yolk
3 tablespoons caster (superfine) sugar
250 ml (9 fl oz/1 cup) milk
500 ml (17 fl oz/2 cups) pouring (whipping) cream
½ teaspoon natural vanilla extract
1 tablespoon demerara sugar

Preheat the oven to 180°C (350°F/Gas 4). Melt 10 g (¼ oz) of the butter and use to brush a 1.5 litre (52 fl oz/6 cup) ovenproof dish. Spread the bread very lightly with the remaining butter and cut each slice in half diagonally. Layer the bread in the prepared dish, sprinkling the cinnamon and sultanas between each layer.

Lightly whisk together the eggs, egg yolk and caster sugar in a large bowl. Heat the milk with the cream until just warm and stir in the vanilla. Whisk the cream mixture into the egg mixture. Strain the custard over the layered bread, then leave for 5 minutes before sprinkling with the demerara sugar.

Bake for 30 minutes, or until the custard has set and the bread is golden brown. Serve warm or at room temperature.

SERVES 4

Pear and apple crumble pie

375 g (13 oz) ready-made
    shortcrust pastry
3 pears, peeled, cored and sliced
4 Granny Smith apples, peeled,
    cored and sliced
60 g (2¼ oz/¼ cup) caster
    (superfine) sugar
2 teaspoons grated orange zest

90 g (3¼ oz/¾ cup) raisins
90 g (3¼ oz/¾ cup) plain
    (all-purpose) flour
95 g (3¼ oz/½ cup) soft brown
    sugar
½ teaspoon ground ginger
90 g (3¼ oz) unsalted butter
whipped cream, to serve

Roll the pastry between two sheets of baking paper until large enough to cover the base and side of a 23 x 18 x 3 cm (9 x 7 x 1¼ inch) pie dish. Remove the top baking paper and invert the pastry into the dish. Trim the excess. Cover with plastic wrap and refrigerate for 20 minutes.

Put the sliced fruit in a large saucepan. Add the sugar, zest and 2 tablespoons of water. Cook over low heat, stirring occasionally, for 20 minutes or until the fruit is tender. Remove from the heat. Add the raisins and a pinch of salt and mix. Cool, then spoon into the pastry case.

Preheat the oven to 200°C (400°F/Gas 6) and heat a baking tray. Combine the flour, brown sugar and ginger in a bowl and rub in the butter until the mixture resembles coarse breadcrumbs. Sprinkle over the fruit.

Place the pie dish on the hot baking tray and bake for 10 minutes. Reduce the oven to 180°C (350°F/Gas 4) and cook for 40 minutes, or until browned. Cover the pie with foil halfway through if the top is browning too quickly. Serve warm with cream.

SERVES 6–8

rich

Mini éclairs

60 g (2¼ oz) unsalted butter, chopped
125 g (4½ oz/1 cup) plain (all-purpose) flour, sifted
4 eggs, beaten
300 ml (10½ fl oz/1¼ cups) pouring (whipping) cream
1 tablespoon icing (confectioners') sugar, sifted
½ teaspoon natural vanilla extract
50 g (1¾ oz) dark chocolate, melted

Preheat the oven to 200°C (400°F/Gas 6). Line two baking trays with baking paper. Put the butter in a saucepan with 250 ml (9 fl oz/1 cup) of water. Stir over low heat until melted. Bring to the boil, then remove from the heat and add all the flour. Beat with a wooden spoon until smooth. Return to the heat and beat for 2 minutes, or until the mixture forms a ball and leaves the side of the pan. Remove from the heat and transfer to a bowl. Cool for 5 minutes. Add the egg, a little at a time, beating well between each addition, until thick and glossy.

Spoon the mixture into a piping bag with a 1.2 cm (½ inch) plain nozzle. Pipe 6 cm (2½ inch) lengths of batter on the trays. Bake for 10 minutes, then reduce the heat to 180°C (350°F/Gas 4) and cook for 10 minutes, or until golden and puffed. Poke a hole into one side of each éclair and remove the soft dough from inside with a teaspoon. Return to the oven for 2–3 minutes. Cool on a rack.

Whip the cream, icing sugar and vanilla until thick. Pipe the cream into the side of each éclair. Dip each éclair into the melted chocolate, face-side-down, then return to the wire rack for the chocolate to set.

MAKES 24

Self-saucing
chocolate pudding

10 g (¼ oz) unsalted butter, melted, plus 50 g (1¾ oz) extra, chopped
75 g (2½ oz) dark chocolate, chopped
125 ml (4 fl oz/½ cup) milk
125 g (4½ oz/1 cup) self-raising flour
4 tablespoons cocoa powder

160 g (5¾ oz/¾ cup) caster (superfine) sugar
1 egg, lightly beaten
115 g (4 oz/½ cup) soft brown sugar
icing (confectioners') sugar, to dust
thick (double/heavy) cream or ice cream, to serve

Preheat the oven to 180°C (350°F/Gas 4). Lightly grease a 2 litre (70 fl oz/8 cup) ovenproof dish with the melted butter.

Put the chopped butter, chocolate and milk in a small saucepan, and stir over medium heat for 3–4 minutes, or until the butter and chocolate have melted. Remove the pan from the heat and allow to cool slightly.

Sift the flour and 2 tablespoons of cocoa, and add to the chocolate mixture with the caster sugar and the egg, stirring until just combined. Spoon into the prepared dish.

Sift the remaining cocoa evenly over the top of the pudding and sprinkle with the brown sugar. Pour 560 ml (19¼ fl oz/2¼ cups) boiling water over the back of a spoon (this stops the water making holes in the cake mixture) over the top of the pudding. Bake for 40 minutes, or until the pudding is firm to the touch. Leave for 2 minutes before dusting with icing sugar. Serve with cream or ice cream.

SERVES 6

Petits pots de crème

400 ml (14 fl oz) milk
1 vanilla bean
3 egg yolks
1 egg
80 g (2¾ oz/⅓ cup) caster (superfine) sugar

Preheat the oven to 140°C (275°F/Gas 1). Put the milk in a saucepan. Split the vanilla bean in two, scrape out the seeds and add the whole lot to the milk. Bring the milk just to the boil.

Meanwhile, mix together the egg yolks, egg and sugar. Strain the boiling milk over the egg mixture and stir well. Skim off the surface to remove any foam.

Ladle into four 25 ml (1 fl oz) ramekins and place in a roasting tin. Pour enough hot water into the tin to come halfway up the sides of the ramekins. Bake for 30 minutes, or until the custards are firm to the touch. Leave the ramekins on a wire rack to cool, then refrigerate until ready to serve.

SERVES 4

Chocolate affogato

250 g (9 oz) dark chocolate
1 litre (35 fl oz/4 cups) milk
6 eggs
110 g (3¾ oz/½ cup) caster (superfine) sugar
340 ml (12 fl oz/1⅓ cup) thick (double/heavy) cream
4 small cups of espresso or very strong coffee
4 shots Frangelico or any other liqueur that you like

Break the chocolate into individual squares and put it with the milk in a saucepan. Heat the milk over low heat. As the milk heats up and the chocolate melts, stir the mixture until you have a smooth liquid. You don't need to boil the milk, as the chocolate will melt at a much lower temperature.

Whisk the eggs and sugar together with electric beaters, in a large glass or metal bowl, until the mixture is pale and frothy. Add the milk and chocolate mixture, along with the cream, and mix.

Pour the mixture into a shallow plastic or metal container and put it in the freezer. In order to make a smooth ice cream you will now have to whisk the mixture every hour or so to break up the ice crystals as they form. When the mixture gets very stiff, leave it to set overnight.

Scoop four balls of ice cream out of the container and put into four cups, then put these in the freezer while you make the coffee.

Serve the ice cream with the Frangelico and coffee poured over it.

SERVES 4

Panna cotta

450 ml (16 fl oz) thick (double/heavy) cream
4 tablespoons caster (superfine) sugar
2 tablespoons grappa (optional)
few drops natural vanilla extract
3 leaves or 1¼ teaspoons gelatine
250 g (9 oz) mixed berries, to serve

Put the cream and sugar in a saucepan and stir over gentle heat until the sugar has dissolved. Bring to the boil, then simmer for 3 minutes, adding the grappa and a few drops of vanilla extract to taste.

If you are using the gelatine leaves, soak them in cold water until floppy, then squeeze out any excess water. Stir the leaves into the hot cream until they are completely dissolved. If you are using powdered gelatine, sprinkle it onto the hot cream in an even layer and leave it to sponge for a minute, then stir it into the cream until dissolved.

Pour the mixture into four 125 ml (4 fl oz/½ cup) metal or ceramic ramekins, cover each with a piece of plastic wrap and refrigerate until set.

Unmould the panna cotta by placing the ramekins very briefly in a bowl of hot water and then tipping them gently onto plates. Metal ramekins will take a shorter time than ceramic to unmould as they heat up quickly. Serve with the fresh berries.

SERVES 4

Walnut pie with caramel sauce

Pastry
250 g (9 oz/2 cups) plain
  (all-purpose) flour
180 g (6½ oz) unsalted butter
40 g (1½ oz/⅓ cup) icing
  (confectioners') sugar
1 egg yolk
3–4 tablespoons iced water

Filling
2 eggs
210 g (7½ oz/1 cup) caster
  (superfine) sugar

150 g (5½ oz/1½ cups) walnuts,
  chopped

1 egg yolk, lightly beaten
icing (confectioners') sugar
walnuts, to garnish

Caramel sauce
40 g (1½ oz) unsalted butter
230 g (8 oz) soft brown sugar
2 teaspoons vanilla extract
200 ml (7 fl oz) pouring
  (whipping) cream

Sift the flour and ½ teaspoon salt into a bowl and rub in the butter. Mix in the icing sugar. Add the egg yolk and water and mix. Lift out and press into a ball. Cover in plastic wrap. Refrigerate for 20 minutes. Preheat the oven to 180°C (350°F/Gas 4). Grease a fluted 36 x 11 cm (14 x 4¼ inch) pie tin.

Beat the eggs and sugar in a bowl. Stir in the walnuts. Divide the dough into two portions. Line the base and side of the tin with one portion. Cover in plastic wrap and refrigerate. Roll out the remaining pastry for a lid. Pour the walnut filling into the shell, brush the rim with egg yolk and cover with the lid. Make a steam hole in the top. Brush with egg yolk and bake for 30–35 minutes. Cool.

To make the sauce, combine the ingredients in a saucepan and cook for 5 minutes, or until thick. Dust the pie with icing sugar and top with the walnuts and sauce.

SERVES 6–8

Creamy chocolate mousse

125 g (4½ oz) dark chocolate, chopped
4 eggs, separated
185 ml (6 fl oz/¾ cup) pouring (whipping) cream, lightly whipped
unsweetened cocoa powder, to serve

Melt the chocolate in a bowl balanced over a saucepan of gently simmering water, making sure the base of the bowl does not touch the water. Stir the chocolate occasionally until it's melted, then take it off the heat to cool slightly. Lightly beat the egg yolks and stir them into the melted chocolate, then gently fold in the cream until velvety.

Beat the egg whites to soft peaks. Fold one spoonful of the fluffy egg white into the mousse with a metal spoon, then gently fold in the remainder.

You only need small quantities of the mousse — you can either serve it in six small wine glasses or 185 ml (6 fl oz/¾ cup) ramekins. Cover with plastic wrap and refrigerate for 4 hours, or overnight until set. When you're ready to serve, add a curl of whipped cream and a dusting of cocoa powder.

SERVES 6

Individual zucotto

450 g (1 lb) packet Madeira cake
3 tablespoons Cointreau
3 tablespoons brandy
300 ml (10½ fl oz) thick (double/heavy) cream
3 teaspoons icing (confectioners') sugar, sifted
80 g (2¾ oz/½ cup) blanched almonds, roasted, roughly chopped
70 g (2½ oz/½ cup) hazelnuts, roasted, roughly chopped
150 g (5½ oz) dark chocolate, finely chopped

Cut the cake into 5 mm (¼ inch) slices. Lightly grease six 150 ml (5 fl oz) ramekins and line with plastic wrap, leaving enough to hang over the sides. Press the pieces of the cake into the ramekins, overlapping to cover the base and sides. Combine the Cointreau and brandy in a bowl. Brush the cake with half the Cointreau mixture.

Put the cream and icing sugar in a bowl, and, using electric beaters, beat until firm and stiff. Fold in the nuts, chocolate and 1½ teaspoons Cointreau mixture. The mixture will be quite stiff.

Spoon the mixture into each ramekin and smooth over the surface. Cover with the overhanging plastic wrap and refrigerate for 2 hours or overnight. To serve, use the plastic wrap to lift the zucotto out of the ramekins, turn upside-down onto serving plates and brush with the remaining Cointreau mixture.

SERVES 6

Cinnamon orange mini pavlovas with berries

2 egg whites
125 g (4½ oz/½ cup) caster (superfine) sugar
2 teaspoons ground cinnamon
1 teaspoon finely grated orange zest
3 teaspoons cornflour (cornstarch)
1 teaspoon white vinegar
125 ml (4 fl oz/½ cup) pouring (whipping) cream
fresh mixed berries, to serve

Preheat the oven to 140°C (275°F/Gas 1). Line a baking tray with baking paper and mark four 10 cm (4 inch) circles. Turn the baking paper upside down so the marks don't stain the meringue.

Beat the egg whites using electric beaters until soft peaks form. Gradually add the sugar, beating well after each addition. Continue to beat for 4–5 minutes, or until the sugar has dissolved and the meringue is thick and glossy. Gently fold in the cinnamon, orange zest, cornflour and vinegar. Place 2 tablespoons of the mixture into each circle, gently spreading it out to the edges with the back of a spoon. Hollow out each centre to make nest shapes.

Bake for 10 minutes, then turn the tray around. Bake for a further 30–35 minutes, or until the pavlovas are pale and crisp. Turn the oven off and leave them to cool completely with the door slightly ajar. The pavlovas may crack slightly on cooling. Whip the cream and spoon a little into each pavlova, top with the berries and serve immediately.

SERVES 4

Sticky date puddings

180 g (6 oz/1 cup) dates, pitted
and roughly chopped
1 teaspoon bicarbonate of soda
(baking soda)
75 g (2½ oz) unsalted butter
155 g (5½ oz/⅔ cup) soft
brown sugar
1 teaspoon vanilla extract
185 g (6½ oz/1½ cups) self-
raising flour, sifted

2 eggs
100 g (3½ oz/1 cup) walnut
halves, roughly chopped

Caramel sauce
155 g (5½ oz/⅔ cup) soft
brown sugar
60 g (2¼ oz) unsalted butter
250 ml (9 fl oz/1 cup) pouring
(whipping) cream

Preheat the oven to 180°C (350°F/Gas 4). Lightly brush six 250 ml (9 fl oz/1 cup) moulds with melted butter and line the bases with circles of baking paper. Put the dates and bicarbonate of soda in a pan and pour in 250 ml (9 fl oz/1 cup) of water. Bring to the boil, remove from the heat and set aside to cool.

Beat the butter, sugar and vanilla with electric beaters until light and creamy. Fold through 1 tablespoon of the flour. Add 1 egg, beat well. Add the other egg and repeat the process.

Fold through the remaining flour, walnuts and date mixture, and mix well. Divide the mixture among the moulds, filling them three-quarters full. Bake for 30–35 minutes, or until slightly risen and firm to the touch.

To make the caramel sauce, put the brown sugar, butter and cream in a pan and simmer for 5 minutes. When the puddings are cooked, remove from the oven and prick a few holes in each one. Drizzle with some of the caramel sauce and return to the oven for 5 minutes. Loosen the side of each pudding with a small knife, turn out, remove the baking paper and serve with the remaining sauce.

SERVES 6

Pistachio crème brûlée

500 ml (17 fl oz/2 cups) pouring (whipping) cream
35 g (1¼ oz/¼ cup) finely chopped pistachios
½ vanilla bean, halved lengthways
½ teaspoon grated orange zest
100 g (3 ½ oz/½ cup) caster (superfine) sugar
5 egg yolks
1–3 tablespoons caster (superfine) sugar, extra
pistachio biscotti, to serve

Preheat the oven to 140°C (275°F/Gas 1). Put the cream, pistachios, vanilla bean, zest and half the sugar in a saucepan over medium heat and stir to dissolve the sugar, then slowly bring to the boil. Remove from the heat and infuse for 10 minutes.

Whisk the egg yolks and remaining sugar in a bowl. Strain the cream mixture into a jug, then add to the egg mixture, stirring continuously. Ladle the custard into six 125 ml (4 fl oz/½ cup) ramekins and place in a roasting tin. Pour in cold water to come halfway up the sides of the ramekins, then place in the oven and cook for 1 hour, or until the custard has set and is only just wobbly. Cool the ramekins on a wire rack, then refrigerate for 4 hours.

Preheat the grill to very hot. Sprinkle 1–2 teaspoons of the extra sugar over the top of each brûlée. Put the brûlées in a roasting tin full of ice, then put the tin under the grill for 4 minutes, or until the tops of the brûlées have melted and caramelized. Remove the ramekins from the roasting tin and dry around the outside edges. Refrigerate for 1–2 hours but not more than 3 hours (or the toffee will start to go sticky and lose its crunch). Serve with pistachio biscotti and some fresh fruit.

SERVES 6

Zabaglione

6 egg yolks
3 tablespoons caster (superfine) sugar
125 ml (4 fl oz/½ cup) sweet Marsala
250 ml (9 fl oz/1 cup) thick (double/heavy) cream

Whisk the egg yolks and sugar in the top of a double boiler or in a heatproof bowl set over a saucepan of simmering water. Make sure that the water does not touch the base of the bowl or the egg may overcook and stick. It is important that you whisk constantly to move the cooked mixture from the outside of the bowl to the centre.

When the egg mixture is tepid, add the Marsala and whisk for another 5 minutes, or until it has thickened enough to hold its shape when drizzled off the whisk into the bowl.

Whip the cream until soft peaks form. Gently fold in the egg and Marsala mixture. Divide among four glasses or bowls. Cover and refrigerate for 3–4 hours before serving.

SERVES 4

Coffee crémets with chocolate sauce

250 g (9 oz/1 cup) cream cheese
250 ml (9 fl oz/1 cup) thick (double/heavy) cream
4 tablespoons very strong coffee
80 g (2¾ oz/⅓ cup) caster (superfine) sugar

Chocolate sauce
100 g (3½ oz) dark chocolate
50 g (1¾ oz) unsalted butter

Line four 100 ml (3½ fl oz) ramekins or heart-shaped moulds with muslin, leaving enough muslin hanging over the side to wrap over the crémet.

Beat the cream cheese a little until smooth, then whisk in the cream. Add the coffee and sugar and mix. Spoon into the ramekins and fold the muslin over the top. Refrigerate for at least 1 hour 30 minutes, then unwrap the muslin and turn the crémets out onto individual plates, carefully peeling the muslin off each one.

To make the chocolate sauce, gently melt the chocolate in a saucepan with the butter and 4 tablespoons water. Stir well to make a shiny sauce, then let the sauce cool a little. Pour a little chocolate sauce over each crémet.

SERVES 4

NOTE: Dark chocolate (also known as plain or bittersweet) is available with different amounts of added sugar. For a really good chocolate sauce, you want to use chocolate with less sugar and more cocoa solids (between 50% and 70%).

Crème caramel

250 ml (9 fl oz/1 cup) milk
250 ml (9 fl oz/1 cup) pouring (whipping) cream
375 g (13 oz/1½ cups) caster (superfine) sugar
1 teaspoon natural vanilla extract
4 eggs, lightly beaten
90 g (3¼ oz/⅓ cup) caster (superfine) sugar, extra

Preheat the oven to 200°C (400°F/Gas 6). Put the milk and cream in a saucepan and gradually bring to boiling point.

Put the sugar in a frying pan and cook over medium heat for 8–10 minutes. Stir occasionally as the sugar melts to form a golden toffee. The sugar may clump together — break up any lumps with a wooden spoon. Pour the toffee into the base of six 125 ml (4 fl oz/½ cup) ramekins or ovenproof dishes.

Combine the vanilla, eggs and extra sugar in a bowl. Remove the milk and cream from the heat and gradually add to the egg mixture, whisking well. Pour the custard mixture evenly over the toffee. Place the ramekins in a baking dish and pour in boiling water until it comes halfway up the sides of the dishes. Bake for 20 minutes, or until set. Use a flat-bladed knife to run around the edges of the dishes and turn out the crème caramel onto a serving plate, toffee-side-up.

SERVES 6

NOTE: When making toffee, watch it carefully as it will take a little while to start melting, but once it starts it will happen very quickly. Stir occasionally to make sure it melts evenly and doesn't stick to the saucepan.

Chocolate croissant pudding

4 croissants, torn into pieces
125 g (4½ oz) dark chocolate,
  chopped into pieces
4 eggs
5 tablespoons caster (superfine)
  sugar
250 ml (9 fl oz/1 cup) milk
250 ml (9 fl oz/1 cup) pouring
  (whipping) cream

3 teaspoons orange liqueur
3 teaspoons grated orange zest
4 tablespoons orange juice
2 tablespoons roughly chopped
  hazelnuts
thick (double/heavy) cream,
  to serve

Preheat the oven to 180°C (350°F/Gas 4). Grease the base and side of a 20 cm (8 inch) deep-sided cake tin and line the bottom of the tin with baking paper. Put the croissant pieces into the tin, then scatter over 100 g (3½ oz) chocolate pieces.

Beat the eggs and sugar together until pale and creamy. Heat the milk, cream and liqueur and remaining chocolate pieces in a saucepan until almost boiling. Stir to melt the chocolate, then remove the pan from the heat. Gradually add to the egg mixture, stirring constantly. Next, stir in the orange zest and juice. Slowly pour the mixture over the croissants, allowing the liquid to be fully absorbed before adding more.

Sprinkle the hazelnuts over the top and bake for 50 minutes, or until a skewer comes out clean when inserted into the centre. Cool for 10 minutes. Turn the pudding out and invert onto a serving plate. Slice and serve warm with a dollop of cream.

SERVES 6–8

Venetian rice pudding

750 ml (26 fl oz/3 cups) milk
250 ml (9 fl oz/1 cup) thick (double/heavy) cream
1 vanilla pod, split
50 g (1¾ oz) caster (superfine) sugar
¼ teaspoon ground cinnamon
pinch grated nutmeg
1 tablespoon grated orange zest
85 g (3 oz) sultanas
2 tablespoons brandy or sweet Marsala
110 g (3¾ oz/½ cup) risotto or pudding rice

Put the milk, double cream and vanilla pod in a heavy-based saucepan, and bring just to the boil, then remove from the heat. Add the sugar, cinnamon, nutmeg and orange zest, and set aside.

Put the sultanas and brandy in a small bowl and leave to soak. Add the rice to the infused milk and return to the heat. Bring to a simmer and stir slowly for 35 minutes, or until the rice is creamy. Stir in the sultanas and remove the vanilla pod at the end of cooking. Serve warm or cold.

SERVES 4

Chocolate pudding

160 g (5¾ oz) dark chocolate, chopped
butter, for greasing
80 g (2¾ oz) caster (superfine) sugar
60 g (2¼ oz) milk chocolate, chopped
4 eggs
pouring (whipping) cream, to serve

Preheat the oven to 200°C (400°F/Gas 6). Put the dark chocolate in a glass bowl and set it above a pan of simmering water. The chocolate will gradually start to soften and look glossy — when it does this, stir it until it is smooth.

Grease the inside of four 200 ml (7 fl oz) ramekins with butter. Add ½ teaspoon of the sugar to each and shake it around until the insides are coated. Divide the chopped milk chocolate among the ramekins.

Beat the rest of the sugar with the egg yolks, using electric beaters, for about 3 minutes, or until you have a pale, creamy mass. Clean the beaters and dry them thoroughly. Whisk the egg whites until they are thick enough to stand up in peaks.

Fold the melted chocolate into the yolk mixture and then fold in the whites. Use a large spoon or rubber spatula to do this and try not to squash out too much air. Divide the mixture among the four ramekins. Bake for 15–20 minutes. The puddings should be puffed and spongelike. Serve straight away with cream.

SERVES 4

Tiramisu

5 eggs, separated
180 g (6 oz) caster (superfine) sugar
250 g (9 oz) mascarpone cheese
250 ml (9 fl oz/1 cup) cold very strong coffee
3 tablespoons brandy or sweet Marsala
44 small sponge fingers
80 g (2¾ oz) dark chocolate, finely grated

Beat the egg yolks with the sugar until the sugar has dissolved and the mixture is light and fluffy and leaves a ribbon trail when dropped from the whisk. Add the mascarpone and beat until the mixture is smooth. Whisk the egg whites in a clean dry glass bowl until soft peaks form. Fold into the mascarpone mixture.

Pour the coffee into a shallow dish and add the brandy. Dip some of the sponge finger biscuits into the coffee mixture, using enough biscuits to cover the base of a 25 cm (10 inch) square dish. The biscuits should be fairly well soaked on both sides but not so much so that they break up. Arrange the biscuits in one tightly packed layer in the base of the dish.

Spread half the mascarpone mixture over the layer of biscuits. Add another layer of soaked biscuits and then another layer of mascarpone, smoothing the top layer neatly. Leave to rest in the fridge for at least 2 hours or overnight. Dust with the grated chocolate to serve.

SERVES 4

Zuppa inglese

4 thick slices sponge or Madeira cake
4 tablespoons kirsch
150 g (5½ oz) raspberries
170 g (6 oz) blackberries
2 tablespoons caster (superfine) sugar
250 ml (9 fl oz/1 cup) custard
250 ml (9 fl oz/1 cup) pouring (whipping) cream, lightly whipped
icing (confectioners') sugar, to dust

Put a piece of sponge cake on each of four deep plates and brush or sprinkle it with the kirsch. Leave the kirsch to soak in for at least a minute or two.

Put the raspberries and blackberries in a saucepan with the caster sugar. Gently warm through over a low heat so that the sugar just melts, then leave the fruit to cool.

Spoon the fruit over the sponge, pour the custard on top of the fruit and, finally, dollop the cream on top and dust with icing sugar.

SERVES 4

Banana cream pie

375 g (13 oz) ready-made
shortcrust pastry
80 g (2¾ oz/½ cup) dark
chocolate chips
4 egg yolks
125 g (4½ oz/½ cup) caster
(superfine) sugar
½ teaspoon vanilla extract
2 tablespoons custard powder

500 ml (17 fl oz/2 cups) milk
40 g (1½ oz) unsalted butter
1 teaspoon brandy or rum
3 large ripe bananas, cut into
3–4 mm (⅛ inch) slices
sliced banana, extra, to
decorate
50 g (1¾ oz) dark chocolate,
grated, to decorate

Roll out the pastry between two sheets of baking paper to line the base of a 23 x
18 x 3 cm (9 x 7 x 1¼ inch) pie tin. Remove the top sheet of paper and invert the
pastry into the tin. Trim the excess. Refrigerate for 20 minutes.

Preheat the oven to 190°C (375°F/Gas 5). Line the pastry with crumpled baking
paper and cover with baking beads or rice. Bake for 10 minutes, remove the paper
and beads, then bake for 10 minutes, or until the pastry is dry and cooked
through. While still hot, cover with chocolate bits. Leave for 5 minutes, then
spread the melted chocolate over the base.

Put the egg yolks, sugar, vanilla and custard powder in a bowl and beat with
electric beaters for 2–3 minutes, or until thick. Bring the milk to the boil in a pan
over medium heat, remove from the heat and gradually pour into the egg mixture,
stirring well. Return the custard filling to the saucepan and bring to the boil,
stirring well. Cook for 2 minutes, or until thick. Remove from the heat, stir in the
butter and brandy and leave to cool. Arrange the banana slices over the chocolate,
then pour over the custard. Decorate with extra banana and the grated chocolate.

SERVES 6–8

Grandmother's
pavlova

4 egg whites
230 g (8 oz/1 cup) caster (superfine) sugar
2 teaspoons cornflour (cornstarch)
1 teaspoon white vinegar
500 ml (17 fl oz/2 cups) pouring (whipping) cream
3 passionfruit, to decorate
strawberries, to decorate

Preheat the oven to 160°C (315°F/Gas 2–3). Line a 32 x 28 cm (13 x 11 inch) baking tray with baking paper.

Place the egg whites and a pinch of salt in a dry bowl. Using electric beaters, beat until stiff peaks form. Add the sugar gradually, beating constantly after each addition, until the mixture is thick and glossy and all the sugar has dissolved.

Using a metal spoon, fold in the cornflour and vinegar. Spoon the mixture into a mound on the prepared tray. Lightly flatten the top of the pavlova and smooth the sides. (This pavlova should have a cake shape and be about 2.5 cm (1 inch) high.) Bake for 1 hour, or until pale cream and crisp. Remove from the oven while warm and carefully turn upside down onto a plate. Allow to cool.

Lightly whip the cream until soft peaks form and spread over the soft centre. Decorate with pulp from the passionfruit and halved strawberries. Cut into wedges to serve.

SERVES 6

Tropical meringues

3 egg whites
175 g (6 oz/¾ cup) caster (superfine) sugar
50 g (1¾ oz/½ cup) desiccated coconut
¼ teaspoon coconut extract
2 tablespoons milk
2 tablespoons caster (superfine) sugar
250 g (9 oz) mascarpone cheese
2 mangoes, peeled and thinly sliced
2 passionfruit

Preheat the oven to 140°C (275°F/Gas 1). Grease and line two baking trays with baking paper.

Put the egg whites in a bowl and whisk until soft peaks form. Add the sugar, 1 tablespoon at a time, until the mixture is glossy. Fold in the desiccated coconut and coconut essence.

Spoon 8 cm (3 inch) mounds of the mixture onto the trays. Bake for 1 hour. Turn the oven off and leave for a further hour.

Add the milk and sugar to the mascarpone and whisk well. Dollop a little onto each meringue and top with the fruit.

MAKES 6

Chocolate and peanut butter pie

200 g (7 oz) chocolate biscuits
(cookies) with cream centre,
crushed
50 g (1¾ oz) unsalted butter
200 g (7 oz/¾ cup) cream cheese
85 g (3 oz/⅔ cup) icing
(confectioners') sugar, sifted
100 g (3½ oz/⅔ cup) smooth
peanut butter
1 teaspoon vanilla extract

250 ml (9 fl oz/1 cup) pouring
(whipping) cream, whipped
3 tablespoons pouring
(whipping) cream, extra
15 g (½ oz) unsalted butter,
extra
50 g (1¾ oz) dark chocolate,
grated
honey-roasted peanuts,
chopped, to garnish

Combine the biscuit crumbs with the melted butter and press into the base and side of a deep 23 x 18 x 3 cm (9 x 7 x 1¼ inch) pie dish and refrigerate for 15 minutes, or until firm.

Put the cream cheese and icing sugar in a bowl and beat using electric beaters until smooth. Add the peanut butter and vanilla and beat. Stir in a third of the whipped cream until smooth, then fold in the remaining whipped cream. Pour the mixture into the pie shell. Refrigerate for 2 hours, or until firm.

Place the extra cream and butter in a saucepan and stir over medium heat until the butter is melted and the cream just comes to a simmer. Remove from the heat, add the grated chocolate, and stir until melted. Cool a little, then dribble the chocolate over the top of the pie to create a lattice pattern. Refrigerate for 2 hours, or until the topping and chocolate are firm. Remove the pie from the fridge, scatter over the chopped peanuts and serve.

SERVES 10–12

Pineapple gratin

800 g (1 lb 12 oz) ripe pineapple, cut into 1.5 cm (⅝ inch) cubes
3 tablespoons dark rum
2 tablespoons unsalted butter
1 teaspoon vanilla extract
45 g (1½ oz/¼ cup) soft brown sugar
½ teaspoon ground ginger
300 g (10½ oz) sour cream
3 tablespoons pouring (whipping) cream
1 teaspoon finely grated lemon zest
95 g (3¼ oz/½ cup) soft brown sugar, to sprinkle, extra

Put the pineapple, rum, butter, vanilla, sugar and ginger in a large saucepan and cook, stirring occasionally, for 8–10 minutes, or until caramelised. Remove from the heat.

Divide the pineapple among four individual gratin dishes and allow to cool slightly.

Combine the sour cream, cream and lemon zest in a bowl, then spoon evenly over the pineapple. Sprinkle the extra sugar over each gratin.

Cook the gratins under a hot grill (broiler) for 4–5 minutes, or until the sugar has melted and caramelised. Take care not to burn them. Serve immediately.

SERVES 4

index

First published in 2008 by Murdoch Books Pty Limited

Murdoch Books Australia
Pier 8/9, 23 Hickson Road
Millers Point NSW 2000
Phone: +61 (0) 2 8220 2000
Fax: +61 (0) 2 8220 2558
www.murdochbooks.com.au

Murdoch Books UK Limited
Erico House, 6th Floor
93–99 Upper Richmond Road,
Putney, London SW15 2TG
Phone: +44 (0) 20 8785 5995
Fax: +44 (0) 20 8785 5985
www.murdochbooks.co.uk

Chief Executive: Juliet Rogers
Publishing Director: Kay Scarlett

Design Manager: Vivien Valk
Project manager and editor: Gordana Trifunovic
Design concept: Alex Frampton
Designer: Susanne Geppert
Production: Kita George
Cover photography: Tanya Zouev
Styling: Stephanie Souvlis
Introduction text: Leanne Kitchen
Recipes developed by the Murdoch Books Test Kitchen

Printed by Sing Cheong Printing Co. Ltd in 2008. PRINTED IN HONG KONG.
Reprinted 2008.

ISBN 978 1 74196 100 3 (pbk.).
A catalogue record for this book is available from the British Library.

IMPORTANT: Those who might be at risk from the effects of salmonella poisoning (the elderly, pregnant women, young children and those suffering from immune deficiency diseases) should consult their doctor with any concerns about eating raw eggs.

CONVERSION GUIDE: You may find cooking times vary depending on the oven you are using. For fan-forced ovens, as a general rule, set the oven temperature to 20°C (35°F) lower than indicated in the recipe. We have used 20 ml (4 teaspoon) tablespoon measures. If you are using a 15 ml (3 teaspoon) tablespoon, for most recipes the difference will not be noticeable. However, for recipes using baking powder, gelatine, bicarbonate of soda (baking soda), small amounts of flour and cornflour (cornstarch), add an extra teaspoon for each tablespoon specified.